Jesus Nation

JESUS NATION

Belonging to and Becoming Part of
the Greatest Nation Ever

Joe Stowell

TYNDALE HOUSE PUBLISHERS, INC.
CAROL STREAM, IL

Visit Tyndale's exciting Web site at www.tyndale.com.

TYNDALE and Tyndale's quill logo are registered trademarks of Tyndale House Publishers, Inc.

Jesus Nation: Belonging to and Becoming Part of the Greatest Nation Ever

Designed by Erik M. Peterson

Library of Congress Cataloging-in-Publication Data

Stowell, Joseph M.
   Jesus nation : belonging to and becoming part of the greatest nation ever / Joe Stowell.
      p. cm.
   Includes bibliographical references (p.   ).
   ISBN 978-1-4143-0049-8 (hc)
1. Christian life—Baptist authors. I. Title.
   BV4501.3.S7699 2009
   248.4′86—dc22   2009022886

Printed in the United States of America

15 14 13 12 11 10 09
 7   6   5   4   3   2   1

With deep appreciation to God for the
wonderful gift of grandchildren, this book is
dedicated to the next wave of Jesus Nationals
who have been born into our family:

Gabriel Joseph
Olivia Grace
Joseph Mishael
Bennett David
Magdalene Cheney
Mary Catherine
Sophia Elisabeth
Silas William
Elijah David
Lily Martha

Contents

ACKNOWLEDGMENTS

AUTHORS ARE LIKE LITTLE KIDS—we need a lot of help. So it wouldn't be right not to tip my hat to those whose names should be on the cover with mine.

A big thanks to Martie, my wife, for her encouragement, insights, and understanding spirit when I disappeared into Computer World to get the manuscript done. I have no idea where my life would be today if God had not blessed me with her friendship and wisdom. She is a gift from God to me in measures that I cannot repay.

Bravo for the good folks at Tyndale House Publishers whose input helped me conceptualize, organize, and finalize the message of this book: Jon Farrar, who has been with me since the beginning, offering insights and suggestions that have taken the book to a higher level; Cara Peterson, whose editorial expertise upgraded the manuscript through the final stages of development; Becky Nesbitt, whose encouragement kept me at it; and Stephanie Krzywonos, who captured the essence of the message in the cover material and helped to brainstorm the articulation of the big idea.

I am indebted to my effectively capable executive assistant, Beth Longjohn, who in her gracious style worked to keep my schedule clear so that I could have space to write. Her management of my life in University World is a blessing beyond description.

But most importantly, I am grateful to Jesus, who has given me something significant to write about. May he be pleased to bless this effort to his glory and the advance of his nation.

INTRODUCTION

Thy Kingdom Come

IF YOU EVER WANTED TO BE an answer to someone's prayer—Jesus' prayer, in particular—this is your chance. Your chance to come to grips with the fact that, as a Christian, you belong to a nation of global and eternal proportions. A nation whose culture and habits are revolutionarily different. A nation that will ultimately prevail over all other nations and offer its inhabitants eternal peace and limitless joy in a new heaven and earth, where there will be "no more death or sorrow or crying or pain" . . . or any of the other twisted and broken stuff that troubles us in this world (Revelation 21:4, NLT). It's a nation that calls all of us who belong to it to live here and now, in our earthside nations, by the radically different habits of the Jesus Nation, so that all can see and experience a preview of the really big show to come. A nation that Jesus prayed for when he prayed, "Thy Kingdom come, Thy will be done in earth, as it is in heaven" (Matthew 6:10, KJV).

A new wave is sweeping the church in the West. Its momentum is driven by a new generation of Jesus followers who are bent on bringing the transforming power of Jesus to a world that is torn by hate, famine, hunger, poverty, injustice, oppression, and war. It calls for the mobilization of men and women to see themselves as agents of global influence. Not just pastors, missionaries, and ministry professionals, but everyone. It's a call to leave our pews and use our talents, treasures, and energies to bring the healing and helping energy of the love of Jesus to people in need both locally and globally.

The motivation is borne out of a fresh awareness of our responsibility to act like people of the Kingdom of God—the Jesus Nation—by bringing the helping hand of Jesus to right wrongs, settle injustices, and feed the poor. This new breed of missionary is committed to bringing clear and clean water to parched and polluted sources; aiding the AIDS crisis by coming to the rescue of children and women who by no choice of their own have been infected; educating the less fortunate and the marginalized; teaching the poor to farm, to fish, and to sustain themselves and their families in other ways; fighting against the evils of the sex-slave trade; and helping to rebuild economies that have been devastated by greed and oppression. And all of this in the name of Jesus.

I can't think of a better way for followers of Jesus to spend their time and talents than to serve the needy and broken as he did. And, in a world that increasingly sees us as troublemakers, bigoted and arrogant in our claims to have the corner on righteousness, truth, and the exclusive claims of Jesus, how better to catch their attention than to show them that this world is a better place because followers of Jesus have mobilized to lend a helping hand?

So, I'm a raving fan of taking the love of Jesus anywhere and everywhere. It's what Jesus Nationals do.

But, if we are not careful, in all the fanfare about our awakened concern for bringing the Jesus Nation to this world, we may miss the eternal and personal ramifications of its agenda in our rush to meet the immediacy of human need.

With his encounter with the woman at the well, Jesus modeled for us the point that human spiritual needs trump human material needs. As he said, he came "to seek and to save the lost" (Luke 19:10). It's not that it's not important to meet material and physical needs in ways that untwist tangled lives in a sin-twisted world. It's just that the eternal destiny of mankind cannot be ignored in the process. We can give them clean water, but as Jesus said, they will thirst again (see John 4:4-26). What people ultimately need is the inner spring of living water that only he can give.

My other concern is that in all of our *doing*, it may be easy to forget the importance of what we are *becoming*. What good is it to transport the light of our good works into a needy world through lives that, at the end of the day, are no different from the lives of any other earth-bound citizen? Or, worse yet, through lives that contradict the claims of Jesus? Living out the national agenda has massive personal ramifications—ramifications that revolutionize how we live. It calls us to become delightfully and refreshingly different. It makes us right-side-up people in an upside-down world. It refocuses our passions and desires from ourselves and pins them squarely on Jesus, our Eternal King and Superhero.

In the end, this book is about our bringing credibility to the message of Jesus by living lives that are just as compelling as our deeds.

Part 1

BEWILDERED

◆

UNDERSTANDING OUR DILEMMA

Chapter 1

THE WAY

IT WAS TO PEOPLE with our kind of hurried-up, messed-up lives that nation-builder Jesus made an incredible statement. He said, "I am the way, and the truth, and the life" (John 14:6). To my way of thinking, he is either a huckster hawking snake oil, or he is onto something.

I say Jesus is onto something! To everyone he encountered, whether rich and successful like Matthew and Luke, whether busy in the routine of life like fishermen eking out an existence at the mercy of the sea, or whether barren and broken by life like a woman at a well, he offered them all something new, something better . . . he offered them *the way.* And when they embraced his solutions, he delivered on the promise of life in a better way. Which makes me think that it's not life that's the problem . . . the problem is that we have not yet found *the way.* That we have not yet embraced his way.

Here is what I find intriguing. Followers of Jesus in the first century were called a lot of things. They were called traitors to Caesar and the empire. They were known as insurrectionists and troublemakers. But to those who knew them best they were known as people of "the Way." Acts 9:2 tells us that the great persecutor, Saul, was hunting down followers of Jesus so that if he found any of "the Way" he could bring them, bound, to Jerusalem. Interestingly, these were people who knew Jesus best, some who knew him personally, and they had found something in Jesus that had given them new hope, new direction, new purpose, and new joy. They had found in Jesus a whole new "way" to live. And it wasn't a passing fancy. They had found something not only worth living for, but worth dying for as well.

Jesus had shown them the way, and they weren't going back!

When we think of Jesus saying that he is the Way, we normally think that is the way to heaven—and he is, for which we are all deeply grateful. But he meant more than that. He meant that he is the way to live. The way to do money, to deal with friends and enemies, to manage our careers, to do family. He meant that he is the way to think, to dream, to desire, to do everything. That his ways are *how we do life,* not just what we do in life. That his ways are just as important as the outcomes . . . in fact, that his ways determine the outcomes. As someone has well said, if you have a WWJD (What Would Jesus Do) bracelet, you should also have a HWJD (How Would Jesus Do it) bracelet, as well. In short, he is the way to become all that he intends us to become.

This is really great news for all of us who feel that there has to be more to our Christianity than we are experiencing. Thousands upon thousands of us have been willing to take the name of Jesus and revel in his grace but have no clue about the adventurous and sometimes radical joy of becoming a person of the Way.

If all you have is the meek, mild Jesus who offers little more than an escape from reality into some ethereal comfort zone that only lasts until you are finished with your devotions, it's no wonder you have yet to find him as a compelling solution to life. You won't know Jesus as he is intended to be known, and life as it is intended to be lived, until you embrace the revolutionary Jesus and the revolutionary realities of the Way. If you are more interested in gaining than in giving; if ideas like "turn the other cheek" seem weak and vulnerable; if losing to win and dying to live seem like propositions for failure; if words like *surrender* and *submission* seem like cowards' words to you; if you fail to see meaning in suffering; if you feel that evil people should get what they deserve, that homeless people should just get a grip, that America is your nation and is totally in the dumps because it is not the "Christian" nation that you thought it should be . . . If this is what your Christianity looks like, then you may have Jesus, but it's clear that he doesn't have you. No wonder you sometimes feel that Jesus hasn't made much of an impact—you're not much different from the average guy who couldn't care less about him.

Instead, let me welcome you to a special journey that fills the moments of your day with a sense of significance and lights your way forward to life on purpose, with a purpose. Let me welcome you to think and live differently. To stop being ordinary and average. To join me and countless others who are learning that life in the "ordinary lane" is not only unnecessary but wasteful, that there is a better way to spend our fleeting years here on this planet.

Chapter 2

SOMETHING'S WRONG

I MUST ADMIT that I am an unrepentant optimist. My glass is always half full and never half empty. In fact, I tilt so far toward the positive that my wife, Martie, says she has to be a pessimist now and then just to keep our lives balanced. But in spite of the delight I take in being positive to a fault, something has been bothering me. After logging a few decades on this planet, I am waking up to the fact that life is not all it's cracked up to be, that in the end, we expect far too much from life as we know it.

In one of my all-time favorite *Peanuts* cartoons, Charlie Brown is standing on the deck of a cruise ship with a disheartened look on his face, clutching his folded deck chair. Lucy, who always seems to have it together, has already unfolded her deck chair and is waxing eloquent about life. Musing aloud, she tells Charlie that some people set the deck chairs of life to look at what has gone by, others set them to look at the here and now, and still others position their chairs to look at what's ahead. To which Charlie responds, "I can't even get my deck chair unfolded."

My guess is that we've all had days when we felt more like Charlie Brown than Lucy. Deep inside, sometimes way down deep inside, there is this nagging feeling that we don't quite have life figured out, that life isn't all we thought it would be. Shouldn't there be something more than the endless to-do lists? Why does the pressure to perform and prosper make us feel like we're chasing the proverbial carrot that's forever dangling in front of us? And why is it that when we take life by the throat and pull off a smashing success, it quickly morphs into mere memory as life trudges on?

If your experience is anything like mine, it doesn't help to buck up and determine that it will be different for you tomorrow. Think of how many times you've decided to take charge and make sure that it all turns out like you want it to, only to have the resolution and determination vaporize as you slowly drift back into life as it has always been.

Why are we too tired, too busy, or too disappointed? Why do dreams rarely materialize, romantic impulses lose their buzz, long-anticipated events rarely measure up? Why are our desires more intriguing than the fulfillment of the desires themselves?

Sure, life has its good times. I'm not totally out on life. In fact, I'd rather be alive than just about anything else! But I do know that hanging around life for any period of time is bound to make us just a little wary about expecting too much. But still we keep searching. We lose ourselves in the latest high-tech toys, get busier climbing the ladder at MegaCorp, take five-star vacations—or wish we could. Still searching, we try to find the holy grail of life in the adrenaline rush of a sexually charged moment or a steamy affair. We attempt to rise above it all by downing an extra drink or two, embarking on spending sprees, taking voyeuristic journeys into Soap-Opera Land or Pornville . . . only to find that when all gets quiet once again we're more empty and haunted than before. As Peter Kreeft observes:

> If we are typically modern, we are bored, jaded, cynical and flat and burnt out. . . . If we were not so bored and empty, we would not have to stimulate ourselves with increasing doses of sex and violence—or just constant busyness. Here we are in the most fantastic fun and games factory ever invented—modern technological society—and we are bored, like a spoiled rich kid in a mansion surrounded by a thousand expensive toys.[1]

If you've ever felt this way, chin up! You're not the only one who has sobered up enough to hear the hollow ring of life pounding in your ears.

Solomon, who had it all—riches, women, fame, wisdom, vast expanses of land, and extravagant palaces—wrote, "I said to myself, 'Come on, let's try pleasure. . . .' I also tried to find meaning by building huge homes for myself. . . . I collected great sums of silver and gold. . . . I hired wonderful singers . . . and had many beautiful concubines. I had everything a man could desire! . . . But as I looked at everything I had worked so hard to accomplish, it was all so meaningless—like chasing the wind" (Ecclesiastes 2:1, 4, 8, 11, NLT).

Woody Allen, inching up to the finish line of life, looked back and mused that life is "like the two trains at the beginning of my movie *Stardust Memories*. There's a train with these gorgeous winners on it, and a train with all the losers in it. You want to be on the train with the winners, but five minutes later, you're pulling into the same depot. My seventy-plus years will be spent better than those of a beggar on the streets of Calcutta. But we'll end up in the same place."

There's nothing like living long enough to see life for what it really is. If you are young, you feel bulletproof. You never think about dying, much less about how life will look to you in the rearview mirror. You believe in the pot of gold at the end of the rainbow. You're certain that if you try hard enough you can swing the heavy mallet at life's county fair and get a free cigar for making the bell ring. There's not a ladder you can't climb. The problem is, as my friend Howard Hendricks is fond of saying, when you get to the top of the ladder, you find that it is leaning against the wrong wall.

So what's the deal with life?

Before you give up on the pursuit of a meaningful life, let me share the good news. Amazingly, God has made a way for us to press the Delete button on all the bad information we get about how to live life according to our instincts, friends, and cultural advisers. His determination to untwist our lives was so deep that he actually showed up here to demonstrate how to make the turn from our self-destructive, disappointing ways. He came to help us reboot our lives and download the right information about friends, enemies, family, career, money, death, suffering, and all the other aspects of existence that tend to confuse and frustrate us. God arrived here on this life-changing mission in the person of Jesus, who pitched his tent among us (see John 1:14), boldly claimed to be "the way" (John 14:6), and promised that if we walked in the way that he walks we could experience life in abundance (see John 10:10).

Before you put this book down with the thought, *So predictable! I knew he'd tell us that Jesus is the answer to life the way it is supposed to be,* give me a chance to explain. There really is something different about life from Jesus' point of view. Something different about seeing ourselves as a part of his Kingdom—his nation. And, even if you've spent your entire life in Church World, you may have missed what he actually means when he claims to have a grip on life the way it is supposed to be. Jesus' spin on life is refreshingly different. In fact, it is revolutionarily different!

A NATIONAL REVOLUTION

Coming to Jesus by believing that God "loves you and has a wonderful plan for your life," does give you hope for something better. He does love you, and he really does have a wonderful plan for your life. But that plan probably is not wonderful in the way you had hoped it would be. If you figured the plan would give you a hall pass on suffering and trouble and set you on your way toward heaven on a downy bed of cash and comfort, then you'll be disappointed.

So let's talk.

If you and I could sit in a quiet place and talk about something important, I would want to talk with you about life, about your life and about mine. After all, my frustrations and disappointments with life are probably not much different from yours.

Even with my bend toward optimism, I am just as tired of the to-do lists that are always "to be continued." I know what it's like to feel that despite all my busyness, I'm not really going anywhere significant. I know what it's like to lack focus and purpose and to feel that all I am doing is swatting flies in the restaurant of life to keep the customers happy. So I don't mean to come across like I have life all figured out. I don't. I know how complex life can become and how tough it is to make sense of it all. Things rarely are simple. You and I are frail. Worse yet, we are fallen. There's no sense kidding ourselves. It's time to stop hiding behind our "everything is fine" masks and get serious about life as it should be, before the "use by" dates on our vital organs have expired.

So what do we do when we finally realize that life is not all it's cracked up to be and, if we can be really transparent, that we're not as cool as we think we are? Well, what you don't do is bail out on the pursuit of life and start living for the moment by doing something that would make what little life you have left even worse. There is a take on life that you may have missed—and in missing that, you have missed what it means to really live. In the end you can take or leave what I am about to tell you, but it just wouldn't be right if I didn't give you a crack at it.

I'm not talking about some hidden cultic formula for living that I discovered in a cave filled with candles, smoke, and incense. Nor do I have another Five Steps to a Wonderful Life routine. We've had enough of those disappointing adventures. Life, relationships, and our inner twistedness are all far too complicated to make a one-size-fits-all solution look really good on each of us.

So here is what I want you to know: Your life can be much more than that blur of random, disconnected events. More than a taffy pull of competing interests that end up leaving you exhausted and restless for a life that is more focused. Your upside-down instincts can be turned right-side up. Life can be a straight shot at an intentional target that all of us can hit, a target worth aiming at. A life in which the detour of experimental behavior doesn't send you to a dead end of regrets. After a smashing success, you don't need to feel empty, wondering what new territory there is to conquer. You never again need to put your head on the pillow at the end of the day, thinking, *There has to be more to life than this!*

Granted, your life will never be perfect . . . here. That's heaven's thrill. We are fallen—fully redeemed and yet not fully redeemed. Your life will never be all that you hope it can be because *you* can never be all that *you* hope you can be. We are all too frail and too fallen. But, though never perfect this side of heaven, belonging to the Jesus Nation and following its revolutionary ways makes all the difference in terms of the meaning and satisfaction that, because of Christ, you can have now.

Rich or poor, winner or loser, blue collar or white, all Jesus Nationals have one thing in common: *Jesus* is stamped on their passports, and his blood has made them fully privileged members of an emerging nation that will ultimately conquer all others and eternally restore peace, joy, justice, and fulfillment for his glory and the nation's gain. And once you belong to this nation, you can begin the joy of untangling your life so that it can become all that he has intended it to be.

HE IS THE WAY

When Jesus said, "I am the way, and the truth, and the life," he meant that he is *the* way (John 14:6). As we have said, it means that he is the way to live. That he came to show us the *way* to handle money, enemies, friends, jobs, families, suffering, and any other challenge we face in life.

God knew we needed something different from life on our own terms, so he welcomed us to believe that he was serious and capable of delivering when he said, "'I know the plans I have for you,' declares the LORD, 'plans to prosper you and not to harm you, plans to give you hope and a future'" (Jeremiah 29:11, NIV).

And Jesus' claim that he came to give us life more abundantly was backed up by three years of tangible evidence. Every time he encountered a life snagged in the dull trap of the ordinary or lives bogged down by the results and regrets of bad instincts. Every time he crossed swords with the proud and self-sufficient or reached out to the loser, the lame, or the lost. When he met the rich young ruler who had lots of stuff but thought that he still didn't have enough. In fact, every time he met anyone, he offered something that person had never known before. Something better than life the way they were living it. And as we now know, this new life begins with an understanding that he died to give us the potential of this life with him on a better plane. Our sinfulness renders us guilty before God and hopelessly separated from Jesus. So Jesus came to do for us what we could not do for ourselves. He paid the penalty for our sins through his death on the cross, so that we could enter into a personal relationship with a holy God and become a part of his nation. And the good news is that it's not an exclusive club. As he clearly said, "Whoever comes to me I will never cast out" (John 6:37). And as Paul affirms, "The wages of sin is death, but the free gift of God is eternal life in Christ Jesus our Lord" (Romans 6:23). And since life in Jesus is a "free gift," it is clear that accepting Jesus as Savior and Lord has nothing to do with your own works. Rather, it's all about his work on the cross for you and your willingness to repent of your sins and to believe that he will receive you to himself as you make him the Lord of your life. As Jesus told an inquiring religious leader of his day, "for God so loved the world, that he gave his only Son, that whoever believes in him should not perish but have eternal life" (John 3:16).

You can be confused about a lot of things, but if you are confused about what it means to live life as a full-fledged member of the Jesus Nation, you are seriously confused. And if your life as a Christian is only a "get out of hell" pass, if your Christianity is fundamentally about the rules, if being a Christian is about being busy for Jesus—if that's all life looks like for you as a follower of Jesus, then, like Charlie Brown, you haven't even begun to set up your deck chair. And be careful, because painting Christianity by the numbers is soon bound to lose its appeal and become routine, which will only make you feel like quitting—or else you'll just hang around Church World like every other grumpy, glazed-over Christian. You know, the kind you always said you didn't want to be!

But if you have a grip on what the Jesus Nation is and what it means to belong and become a loyal follower of its King, then you will be on a lifelong adventure that you will never regret. It will fill your life with focus, fulfillment, and purpose, and it will give you something better and bigger to live for than just yourself and your fleeting fancies and dissolving triumphs.

Chapter 3

CUBS NATION

I AM A CHICAGO CUBS FAN . . . to the death! In my mind, there is nothing quite like showing up on a bright summer day at the Friendly Confines of Chicago's Wrigley Field to cheer on the Cubbies. And I'm not alone. Strangely enough, the Cubs draw capacity crowds regardless of the fact that they rarely win anything significant. I guess to some of us they wouldn't be our Cubs if they didn't disappoint us! In fact, as I am writing this chapter, they have just lost three in a row in the play-offs after being the best team in the National League all season. So now my Cubs are going on their 101st year of not winning the World Series. But regardless, I love the Cubs! And for years I have been proud to simply be known as an individual who is cheering for the Cubs.

Until, that is, I began hearing people talk about the Cubs Nation. Cubs Nation. Hmm! It had a nice ring to it. It sounded bigger and better than simply being a stand-alone Cubs fan. It sounded like the kind of group you'd want to belong to—if you were a Cubs fan, that is. To be in the Cubs Nation means that you are no longer alone in your quest for baseball's ultimate prize, that you belong to a group and a cause that is bigger than yourself. You are part of a nation that is as diverse as the city of Chicago itself. Whether you are rich or poor, old or young, speak with an accent or not, you belong to this special nation. Those of us in the Cubs Nation believe in the same thing. We are committed to the same cause. We are happy to sit with strangers, to high-five people we've never met in moments of victory, and to commiserate together in moments of defeat. We even have a national anthem: "Go, Cubs, go! Go, Cubs, go! Hey, Chicago, what do you say? The Cubs are gonna win today!" And when it's time for the seventh-inning stretch, the stadium is alive with nationals swaying and singing, "Take me out to the ball game!" It's a massive movement, and it's way too cool.

But you have to experience it to know the thrill of it all.

A DAY IN CUBS NATION

It was a perfect summer day, except for the fact that the Cubbies were in midsummer doldrums. I took my seat in the second deck above first base, hoping that our superhero first baseman, Derrek Lee, who had been reactivated the day before, would be occupying his usual position just below my seat. To my dismay, he didn't take the field. As the game progressed, it looked as if it would be like a lot of other days at Wrigley: a beautiful day but with another loss looming on the horizon.

There wasn't much joy in the Cubs Nation going into the ninth inning. We were behind by three runs. But, just when all hope seemed lost, the Cubbies loaded up the bases. Since the end of the batting order was up, it was easy to feel that our hopes would soon be dashed. Just as I'd given up hope for a Cubs win, who should emerge from the dugout but slugger Lee! The place went wild. But not nearly as wild as the outbreak of deafening delight when Derrek smacked the ball out of the park for a grand slam, handing the Cubs an undisputed win! Just in the nick of time—just when all seemed lost—our hero emerged to defeat the enemy and hand the victory over to the nation. We were sure losers, all of us, until he showed up. He did for us what we couldn't do for ourselves, as we all basked in the spoils of victory, arm in arm, rocking the stadium with repeated refrains of, "Go, Cubs, Go."

Moms who had brought their kids to the game to get out of the house, women in sundresses who had come to enjoy a day in the warm rays, businesspeople who had spent the game in skyboxes negotiating deals, bare-chested bleacher bums, and the brats-and-beer crowd were, in that moment, lifted above personal differences. We all belonged to the winning team, we all belonged to each other, and all the cares and concerns of life were eclipsed by the moment.

If you belong to Cubs Nation, you are never ashamed. Even in times of defeat, we proudly sport Cubswear: T-shirts, caps, sweatshirts, and Windbreakers. And true nationals show up in all kinds of places with our favorite player's jersey on. Belonging to Cubs Nation means that we cheer at the same time for the same things and agonize together over injustices inflicted on us by home-plate umpires. We have a unique way of looking at winning and losing, and we talk about different things than they do in Milwaukee, Cleveland, and Boston. In short, we belong to a nation that has impacted our heads and forever taken our hearts. And regardless of the overwhelming odds, we believe with an unshakable confidence that the day is coming when we will win the ultimate championship and be vindicated for our loyal allegiance to the Cubs Nation.

We courageously enter hostile territory as our team takes to the road. We proudly sit among people of the Cardinal Nation in St. Louis, without wincing or retreating from our undaunted allegiance. Win, lose, or draw, we belong to the Cubs Nation, and we are more than happy to live like it.

But what I really like about the idea of a Cubs Nation is that it has finally given me a way to express the essence of authentic Christianity. Whether you like baseball or not, when you understand the dynamics of the Cubs Nation, it will help you get to where Jesus wants you to be in the game of life. The metaphor speaks to the joys of *belonging* to something bigger and more significant than ourselves. Something worth cheering for. Something worth being proud of. Something with a compelling purpose that we can embrace. And something that propels us to *become* what Jesus intends us to become. It's revolutionary, in the best sense of the term.

There is something about thinking in terms of belonging to the Jesus Nation that works. Across all lines of class, color, language, location, and income, we have something far more important in common than the differences that divide us. We find ourselves rooting for a common cause and celebrating the same hero. Together we are undaunted and unashamed, willing to go together, arm in arm, into hostile territory if necessary. Like people of any other nation, we have a distinct culture and national habits that clearly identify us as members of the Jesus Nation. And, while we are certainly more involved in the advance of the "national agenda" than fans at a ballpark are, it is true that there are times when we watch intently and cheer on those who are called to take to the field on behalf of the cause. And, like managers flashing coded signals, there are dynamics that are hidden from us by unseen forces who are managing the nation as it moves inevitably to the championship that has been assured by the completed work of our Superhero, Jesus.

LIVING OUT OUR NATIONAL IDENTITY

Given the uniqueness of the Jesus Nation, we are different from others—really different—and, as such, clearly identifiable.

So if you think about your career like everyone else . . . of money like everyone else . . . of your enemies like everyone else . . . of sex like everyone else . . . of your family like everyone else . . . of the use of power like everyone else . . . of the poor and oppressed like everyone else, then you have yet to understand what it means to belong to the Jesus Nation. If you think of yourself primarily as an American, an African American, a Latino, a European, an Asian, a Middle Easterner; if you think of yourself primarily as a Methodist, Baptist, Presbyterian, Lutheran, Episcopalian, Catholic, or whatever it says over the door of your church, then you have yet to embrace your identity as a Jesus National.

And if you're wondering if it's worth it to get charged up about the Jesus Nation, think again. There are really only two nations. As God's Word says, it's either the domain of darkness where Satan reigns, or it's the nation of Jesus (see Colossians 1:13). They both have a culture and habitual practices that mark the nationals that inhabit their territory. We only have two choices: life by the Lord of Destruction, or life by King Jesus. Take your pick! And for those of us who have not really thought much about belonging to the Jesus Nation but think of ourselves as good, rule-keeping Christians, beware! It is possible to have been given a passport and redemptive visa into the Jesus Nation by the King himself and yet continue to live by the habits and cultural ways of the domain of darkness.

It's easy to be deceived here. You might be thinking, *I'm not like* them. *I don't sleep around; I go to church, tithe, pay my taxes, and have blocks on my computer that keep pornography at bay.* Those kinds of things are obvious when you think of yourself as a mere Christian. But while those things are worthy of a few spiritual attaboys, here's the point: If that's all there is, you have yet to fully embrace your place in the Jesus Nation, and you will inevitably live with the haunted feeling that even though you're a Christian, something is missing, something is wrong. Your life and, in particular, your Christianity are less than you had expected.

For years, I have been trying to tell anyone who will listen that we are more than mere Christians. To see ourselves as simply having beaten the rap on hell and started on our way to heaven is missing the point. When Jesus brought us to himself, he signed us up to join a revolution of major proportions, a nation in the making. Our hero, Jesus, has emerged from the dugout just in the nick of time and has handed our enemy a significant—ultimately eternal—defeat. And because he has won on our behalf, we, too, are winners.

But if you have little or no sense of belonging to a great and glorious cause far larger than yourself; no common togetherness with Jesus; no mutual allegiance to thinking, acting, and looking really different, as he is really different; and no pride in marking your life with the cause that in the end (unlike my Cubs) will pull off an absolutely hands-down-no-questions-asked win, then you have missed the very essence of authentic Christianity.

To be honest, after hanging around Church World for most of my life, I've clearly seen that a lot of us have missed the essence of what it means to be a Christian. And I have seen that when we don't realize that we have been called to not only belong to Jesus but also become active participants in his revolutionary cause, we become dull and disillusioned; and we wonder why our Christian life is so much less than it ought to be.

Chapter 4

CLUELESS

MARCI WAS IN HER MID-FIFTIES. Although this season of her life was less stressful than earlier seasons, its downside was a sense of loss and futility. Busy days drowned out her troubling thoughts, but in the quiet times they were still there. She had a good marriage and good kids, but they were now gone from home. Even the happy prospect of grandkids was squelched by the fact that they would probably live so far away that she would not be an important part of their lives.

What bothered Marci was the feeling that life had just been a loosely connected sequence of necessities and urgencies, running here and there to make sure her husband and children were well cared for and that the home front stayed intact. She hadn't given much thought to the deep meaning of it all; her life had been driven more by survival than purpose. In fact, she was too busy to think about much of anything . . . until now. And now she felt empty and insignificant.

It didn't help that her husband was a hugely successful corporate leader known globally for his management prowess. Marci had all the money she wanted, but money was the last thing she wanted—most of the time, anyway. What she wanted was to believe that her life had significance and destiny. She felt trapped by a world that says significance is found in public performance and the gold goes to the one who gets the biggest applause while dancing on the stage of life.

Marci felt selfish and inwardly preoccupied whenever she processed her thoughts. She worried that God would not be pleased with her feelings, but then what did he expect? She had tried to keep her spiritual life in good order through all the years and to work hard like a good Christian should. She had volunteered in the nursery and sung on the worship team. But all that didn't seem to count for much anymore.

She felt alone and empty.

She wondered if the feminist revolution, which she had persistently refused to join, had a point after all. She should have gotten a career and made something of her life! Her friend Heather had done just that. But Marci had always considered Heather selfish, cheating her family by giving the best hours of her day to her job—and she thought that Heather was somehow less spiritually sharp for her decision. Now, though, what really nagged Marci was the fact that in spite of all the pressure, Heather had pulled it off in the end. She was Superwoman! Marci never felt like a superwoman.

Over one of those decadently expensive cups of coffee, Heather surprised Marci by sharing that her life had left her second-guessing her own choices too. Being a highly celebrated woman in the ranks of upper management hadn't been all it was cracked up to be. She admitted to being haunted by second thoughts about her choices.

Marci left the get-together thinking, *What on earth is life all about, anyway?*

Marci wondered what she had missed. The truth was that she had missed the revolution, and Heather was now wondering if maybe she had joined the wrong revolution. So, when a good friend in their small group told them that there was a revolution in process, a nation in the making, they were intrigued. It didn't sound very feminine, but something inside Marci and Heather wanted to rise up and conquer. The thought of a radical revolution had a compelling draw . . . maybe their restless souls could find meaning and significance after all.

Josh had watched a lot of adults, including his mom and dad. They were good people, and although they went to church, they were not much different from the nonchurched parents of his friends. Do the chores, keep up with the Joneses, go to work, come home, watch TV, go to bed, and start all over again the next day.

His high school and college teachers had taunted him about his Christianity, convincing him that belief in God was an outdated form of superstition that worked as a crutch for the weak. Life was really what you made of it. His friends were into the good life. Life to them was about their music and experimentation with drinking, drugs, and sex.

Josh joined the crowd.

Josh was now twenty-eight years old. His friends had scattered, and he was struggling to recover from life in the make-ourselves-happy lane. A lot had changed for the better, but he was still trying to get a grip on what life should really be all about. He had a pretty good job. He was back in church again but still hearing the same old thing: "Get busy for God!" "Stay in the Word!" "Behave!" "Believe!" All good stuff, but he kept asking himself, *Doesn't God have anything to say to my heart's cry for a life that will count for something besides stars on my spiritual chart?*

Josh often wondered why church people seemed to be all about the church programs, services, and whether or not they liked the preaching. It seemed like church was a lot like everything else: about me and what I like and don't like. About what I need to make me feel better about myself and to find an easy path to navigate life's struggles. He wondered why Jesus seemed like such a sidebar. Why it wasn't more about him.

Josh loved what he knew about Jesus. He often read through the Gospels, watching Jesus at work. He found Jesus to be strong, humble, revolutionary—the real deal. Unhindered by tradition and man-made rules, Jesus seemed fresh to him. Followable. He just didn't know how to make that kind of Jesus work in his life. He didn't see much of Jesus at church, not in the congregation or even in the leaders. He wondered what would be different about church if Jesus were the senior pastor . . . or the janitor, for that matter.

He had tried to talk to some of the church folk about these thoughts, but he got the feeling that they looked at him as a young idealist and that they smugly knew a secret. You know, the secret that, when Josh matured a little, he would get over it and be just like them. But that was the last thing he wanted to have happen.

What Josh longed for was all wrapped up in the Jesus Nation. But he didn't even know there was one. No one had ever told him that he could find authenticity and something worth living for if he would realize that he didn't simply belong to Jesus but to the nation that bears his name. Why hadn't anyone told him? Could it be that no one in his church or circle of friends really knew?

And then there was Dan. He worked hard at his career and advanced further than he had ever thought he would. With retirement not too far away, like a lot of guys his age, Dan periodically glanced at life through the rearview mirror. He wondered how his wife, Marci, would be doing if he had made her the priority that she deserved to be, if he had slowed his career momentum to pour his time and attention back into her and the kids, particularly Josh, who seemed so loose and disconnected.

Dan had served as an elder for years at church and was well thought of by everyone. But he was troubled inside. As his life and career began to peak, it seemed that he could see more clearly. He was nagged by the thought that his great corporate success had really been all about him and that very few, if any, of his associates would think that Dan had worked for anything other than the advancement of his own career and financial gain. After all, that's what all of them lived for. Why should Dan be different? He had loved to bask in the limelight, and he ate up the applause. But now he felt small for feeling so big, as though it had been all about him. He wished he could have the years back.

He never talked to Marci or Josh about how he really felt deep within. He just kept pouring himself back into his work. It was all he knew how to do . . . and the adrenaline helped keep him from thinking too deeply. He had no clue how to ramp off the corporate highway onto a road that was more lastingly meaningful.

We're all running out of time. But staying clueless dooms our lives to disillusionment at best, perhaps even despair. There is a lot at stake. Getting a grip on belonging to the Jesus Nation will help us to know that at the end of the day—before we get to the end of our lives—the most important thing is Jesus. But not just knowing him or knowing about him. He calls us to action, to live by his wise ways, to follow him into his world—the revolutionary world of his emerging nation.

RIDIN' THE CANNONBALL EXPRESS!

IT WAS ONE OF THOSE middle-of-the-night moments when you turn over in bed, and instead of letting you peacefully drift off again, your brain gets in gear. For some reason I began thinking about all the places that the journey of my life had taken me. I'm not much for having visions. In fact, I don't claim to be so important that God would choose me out of the six billion people that live here on earth to do me the favor of a special appearance. But it was kind of like a vision . . . or maybe just a vivid picture.

As I glanced into the rearview mirror, my past looked a lot like a train ride. In the early years my mom, dad, sisters, and Jesus were all on the ride with me. The first major stop was High School Station, where sports, friends, dating, and an occasional encounter with academics occupied my time. Four years later, I was back on board again and headed toward College Station. As the engine pulled away, I looked back and saw all my high school buddies waving good-bye. My mom, dad, and sisters were now for the most part off the train. My four-year stop at college was busy with campus leadership, clubs, more sports, more academics, and generally having a blast living on the edge of getting caught. It was there that I saw this drop-dead gorgeous woman wandering around campus unprotected. Thinking that someone should volunteer for guard duty, I asked her if I could give her the protection she deserved by spending a lot of time with her. Thankfully, she seemed to think that it was a good idea! When the whistle blew, I asked if she wanted to get on the train with me. She agreed, and as we started down the track, I looked back to see all my teachers, coaches, and friends waving good-bye, knowing that I would never see most of them again.

Seminary was next. Those four years came and went, and then Martie and I and our first son got on board, and we waved good-bye to godly professors who had deeply impacted my life and colleagues who shared our vision and passion for doing something important for God through our lives. Then it was off to our first church. A few years later, we were on our way again, with two more kids in tow as the train pulled into another Church Station, and then another. Leaving again, we waved good-bye to people we loved and went on our way to Moody Bible Institute, where our stay would last for nearly eighteen years. And then we were off again, waving good-bye to all those good people and great students, with a brief stop to serve as a teaching pastor and then back on board again, headed for another College Station, Cornerstone University. How long I'll be on the Cornerstone University platform I'm not quite sure, but the day will come when I get back on board, with my train moving like a cannonball express toward its next destination.

LESSONS FROM THE RIDE

Thinking of my life like this, I found myself pondering some really important thoughts. Thoughts that brought clarity and motivated me to see life in a whole new light. Thoughts that made me want to embrace what it means to belong to the Jesus Nation in a fuller, more meaningful way, and to become all that I aspire to become as a devoted follower of him.

So, here are my life-clarifying thoughts:

- Life is fast, and before you know it, you've traveled a long way.
- The platforms are important stops, but they are not the most important things in your life.
- What is ultimately important is the faithful group of people who travel on the journey with you: your spouse, your kids, and Jesus. And if you are single, it's a few tight friends, family, and Jesus. You'd better not let what is happening on the platform distract you from the people who really count.

- Since there are only a few who will be traveling all the way with you, pour your life into them. All the "platform people" come and go. As important as they seem at the time, they are not the most important thing about the journey.
- If for some reason your spouse and kids detrain—if your friends and family don't get back on with you—Jesus is still there. Jesus is the only one guaranteed to go all the way across the border with you. And with him on your train, there'll be no hassle at the checkpoint. So, above all else, pour your life into *him*—or, better yet, let him pour his life into you. To ignore him, take him for granted, or neglect him for the seductive distractions on the platforms of life is not only shortsighted but dangerous.

Let me explain the dangerous part. Dangerous, because left to ourselves, to our own instincts and desires, we tend to self-destruct.

NUMBERING OUR DAYS

I got out of bed that morning with the prayer of Psalm 90:12 on my mind: "Teach us to number our days that we may get a heart of wisdom." I decided to get my Bible out and read the whole chapter. I had read through the psalm before, but this time something struck me as being significant.

What caught my attention was that the preceding verses spoke of God's wrath and judgment in the context of the length of our years and our need for wisdom. This is the danger zone. The psalmist wrote, "For all our days pass away under your wrath; we bring our years to an end like a sigh. The years of our life are seventy, or even by reason of strength eighty; yet their span is but toil and trouble; they are soon gone, and we fly away. Who considers the power of your anger, and your wrath according to the fear of you?" (Psalm 90:9-11). It was with these thoughts ringing in his heart that the psalmist was propelled to ask God to help him be aware of the brevity of his life so that he would live wisely.

For years I took this verse to mean that living wisely in light of our brief lives was intended to help us each give a good account to God when we reach our expiration dates. An important thought! But, in light of the context of the judgment of God, a whole new thought surfaced that

27

brings into focus a critical tension. The existence of this tension helps me understand why life seems so messed up and dangerous without Jesus. Why life seems out of sync when we don't know that we belong to his nation. Why we have not yet discovered that we can become all we have really wanted to become when we surrender to his wisdom. The wisdom that shapes the nation's culture.

So let's connect the dots.

There is only one place in Scripture where length of life and God's wrath and judgment are in tension. It is in the very early stages of history when, as Scripture reports, people lived for centuries. Literally! Just read Genesis 5. People used to live for eight or nine hundred years. Think of it: If we had that life span, we could sit around and say, "Do you remember what you were doing when Columbus discovered America?" or "Aren't you glad that we don't live in medieval times anymore?" But the problem with having people live that long was that, given our frailty and fallenness, sin and its effects on society grew exponentially more destructive. The longer humanity lived, the worse we became.

When lives are driven by unwise, fallen instincts, they unravel—and they unravel in a really bad way if you live for eight centuries. So God reduced the number of our days to save us from ourselves. In other words, when we "number our days" and realize that it's no longer eight hundred but perhaps eighty years, we are reminded that God had to shorten our life span because of our lack of wisdom and our bent toward sinfulness.

Here's the deal. Left to ourselves and our own instincts, we have the potential to do a lot of harm. Think of greed and hate escalating for centuries. Of the damage that affairs inflict on family, friends, and communities spinning out of control for three hundred years. Think of the devastation that wars lasting for centuries would bring. Think of the toxic fumes of selfishness, bitterness, deceit, and perversion compounding for nearly a millennium, and you begin to get God's point. He needed to cap the damage potential, so he capped our shelf life.

The implication in the psalmist's prayer is that we are not instinctively wise. That left to ourselves we will live unwisely, and if we are left to ourselves long enough, we might just self-destruct. Therefore, an awareness of our days' needing to be numbered is a clear reminder that we desperately need help.

Actually, the psalmist is letting us in on a great secret: The problem with life is not life at all. The problem is us. On our own, we don't know how to "do" life.

One thing is certain: We are born with the DNA of sin deeply embedded in our souls, we are broken from the get-go. We instinctively act and react in wrong and harmful ways. We are born with an obsessive addiction to ourselves and therefore find it difficult to navigate our way through a world of people who collide with our desires and dreams. We are like blind people accelerating through a traffic jam.

That explains why we lead such ready-fire-aim lives. In fact, we're a lot like the village idiot who prided himself on being a great shot. The secret to his success was that after he shot his arrow at the side of a barn, he would paint a target around the arrow—with the bull's-eye centered on the arrow.

But the bull's-eye of life is not our "I want my life to be like this, thank you" barn-side paintings. The ultimate bull's-eye is already painted in the brushstrokes of God's wisdom, and that is why as fallen, frail people we miss the target regularly. By our very nature we are sinful and wrongheaded.

I have come to realize that my first instincts in a given situation are probably wrong. If you don't quite get this, then let me ask you if, when you are deeply offended, your first instinct is to "turn the other cheek"? Is your first thought, *Let's see, how can I love and forgive my offender?* Probably not. The twist is that wrong instincts don't always feel wrong. It seems right to get even, to stash away as much money as I can, to make sure that I am recognized and affirmed, to seek pleasure for myself, to live life to the fullest on my own terms, to do everything to dodge suffering and resent it when it invades my life, to try to be as strong as I can because only the strong survive, and to yell at people who yell at me. But here is the warning about living by the counsel of instincts that most often go south: God says, "There is a way that seems right to a man, but its end is the way to death" (Proverbs 14:12).

So, the problem is not life, after all. The problem is us! As Pogo the comic-strip character said, "We have met the enemy, and he is us!" I've discovered that life's disappointments have a way of proving that there is something wrong with me. When I'm bumped by life, stuff I'm not very proud of tends to spill out.

Even traffic can prove how out of whack we are.

Running late, a woman was stuck behind one of those cautious drivers, the kind that hopes that green lights will turn red. Convinced that she could have made it through the intersection as the light turned yellow, she began honking her horn, screaming at the man driving the car in front of her and punctuating with a gesture or two. Suddenly there was a knock at her window, and a stern-looking policeman asked her to step out of the car, handcuffed her, and took her to the police station, where she was fingerprinted and placed in a holding cell.

Hours later the policeman opened the cell door and led her out, returned her belongings, and sheepishly apologized. He explained, "When I saw you screaming at the man in front of you and flipping him off, I noticed the chrome fish symbol mounted on your trunk and your 'Follow Me to Sunday School' and 'Restore Prayer in School' bumper stickers."

"Ma'am," he finished, "I assumed you had stolen the car."

I guess I get a kick out of that story because there are parts of me that can identify with how she felt and reacted. There she was, decked out with all the right bumper stickers and symbols of what she wanted her life to look like. Until, that is, life got in the way and she flipped into overload. When that happens, you can usually forget the bumper stickers and wake up to what the real you looks like. I've done a lot of things that have caused me to have "out of body" experiences, where I find myself saying, "Stowell, was that really you?" To which the answer is, "Unfortunately, yes!"

So let's fess up! We need help. And according to the psalmist, the help we need is wisdom. Because we are bent in the wrong direction, we are in desperate need of God's wisdom to live right. We need life-changing wisdom in order to live life on this speeding train the way it is supposed to be lived.

Where is that wisdom found?

In Jesus, the one who is going all the way with you! This is why Paul desires that our hearts be "encouraged . . . to reach all the riches of full assurance of understanding and the knowledge of God's mystery, which is Christ, in whom are hidden all the treasures of wisdom and knowledge" (Colossians 2:2-3). Jesus holds the key to life. The key to the wisdom to manage life the way it is supposed to be lived. But here is the rub, if I can say it again: His wisdom will not always seem right to you. He says weird, counterintuitive things like "Turn the other cheek," "Die so that you can live," "Give to gain," "Forgive the same offense 490 times," "Love your enemy," and "Suffer with a joyful spirit!" Sound upside down to you? Sure it does. But it sounds that way not because Jesus is upside down but because you are upside down.

In a biblical sense, given our bent toward wrongness, we are a mess. Ever get up in the morning and slather a piece of toast with butter and then spread a quarter-inch layer of jam on it? Why toast leaps out of our hands, I'll never know. But the greater mystery is why it always lands upside down and makes such a mess. Left to ourselves, we are upside-down toast. Jesus has come like a divine spatula to turn us right-side up and clean up the mess of our lives by giving us the right-side-up wisdom for life. And it is this wisdom that drives and defines the behavior patterns of the Jesus Nation. When we live by Jesus' wisdom, we are safe from the danger of ourselves. Safe—but not trouble free. Living as a Jesus National does not exempt us from struggling. It advises us with Jesus' wisdom on how to navigate the whitewater of life in a foreign place.

Thankfully, Jesus was no pie-in-the-sky nation builder who thought that he should wave his divine wand and make this world a wonderful place, granting all who would follow him unbridled happiness in the here and now. Fixing this messed-up world might be an extreme makeover, but it would never be perfect like it was in Eden. So he determined that when the time was right he would start over and create a new heaven and a new earth. But until then, he is well aware that as long as we live in this world, we will have some pretty significant struggles. Which is why he warned his disciples, "In this world you will have trouble" (John 16:33, NIV). There is no getting around the fact that as long as we live in a fallen place as a part of a fallen race life will frequently be headed for the dump. But Jesus concludes that verse above with these words of affirming hope: "But take heart! I have overcome the world."

Our champion, Jesus, is leading us as freed captives over treacherous terrain against the opposition of spiritual powers in high places. But remember, since he's leading the procession, it's the victory procession of the Jesus Nation! With every step forward, he leads us to live in overcoming ways with the power of his wisdom and his amazing perspectives on life in enemy territory.

Life is short, and there are lots of stops and distractions along the way. So as it speeds along, be sure to stick with Jesus, the King of Wisdom. Our fleeting days need to continually remind us that we are not as bright as we think we are, and that because we live in a fallen place in the midst of a fallen race, we desperately need him.

Chapter 6

A NATION AT RISK

HIS NAME IS BEN, and he rules the island. He's intelligent, crafty, and slick. No one quite knows his full intentions, but it's clear as you watch the blockbuster TV show *Lost* that he is dangerous and that his intentions for anyone who ends up on his island are not good.

The survivors of Oceanic Air flight 815 set up camp on the beach where their plane has crashed only to realize that they are not alone on the island. Hoping that the islanders will be their ticket to rescue, they find instead that the intention of Ben and "the Others" are not to help them but to lure them into Ben's schemes. Eerie supernatural noises and strange dark sightings begin to strike fear into their otherwise brave hearts, and it quickly becomes apparent that until the survivors are rescued, they are going to have to live in hostile territory in wise and careful ways. Most important, they will have to stay tight in loyal and supportive relationships given the danger that they face. Because, worst of all, they are stuck there.

It's hard to think of a more compelling picture of what we are up against when we finally realize that we belong to the Jesus Nation. We are all survivors of the worst crash landing in all of history: the fall of mankind and creation. There is a dark force who roams freely around our "island." He's a lot like Ben: intelligent, crafty, and bent on using anyone in his reach to advance his schemes. But the danger is not always overt.

On the show, "the good life" with Ben stands in sharp contrast to the meager rations and resources that the survivors have to share among themselves. It appears that these islanders hold all the cards, so it wouldn't have been surprising if the survivors had wanted to join them. But the wiser ones resist the temptation, instead focusing on maintaining their unique identity and living wisely in light of the eventual airlift rescue that they keep looking for.

Of course, we have a similar history.

OUR "ISLAND"

In the beginning, our "island" wasn't a hostile place at all. God made the universe as a backdrop for a splendid garden called Eden, a massive stretch of land that became home to the earth's first inhabitants. As spectacular as this Garden was, the most wonderful experience of all was that God, its Creator, in all his glory, actually walked in it with Adam and Eve, not as a taskmaster or grand inspector but as a friend. He had made Adam and Eve in his image so that there could be the joy of uninterrupted and intimate companionship between God and his creation. And it was perfect! No sin. No domestic quarrels. No bad hair days. No fear. No pain. No sorrow. No loss. Just Adam, Eve, and God in perfect harmony in a fabulous place. Satisfying? To say the least! It's hard to imagine—actually impossible to fully imagine.

I love beautiful gardens and the sight of green rolling hills and valleys washed with sunshine and warm breezes. Martie and I have thoroughly enjoyed walking through some of England's most brilliant gardens. Believe me, the fragrances, colors, and designs of these well-manicured layouts are beyond description. You've got to be there to appreciate the experience. And this is after the fall of the universe with all the inflicted damage of the fallout of sin (see Romans 8:18-23). So I often reflect, *If our world and all of God's creation is so stunning now, think of what it must have been like in Eden.*

For instance, think of the joy of those rare days when there is deep, satisfying joy in just being with friends or family. You can't beat the laughter, storytelling, warmth, and love, but the next morning, you have to go to work; yesterday is only a good memory. Think of the richness of such experiences going on forever, without your having to go to work! Think of those times when God has seemed so near to you, when his Word has been so fresh and rewarding and his fellowship so sweet. But then life goes on, and the distance of God seems immeasurable. There was none of that distance in the Garden. He was there 24/7, and a soul-satisfying intimacy with the Creator was a full-access privilege.

Until the day that the Evil Lord of Destruction—Satan—slithered onto the scene and wound his seductive self around the branches of the tree to tempt Eve with the forbidden fruit.

THE CRASH

Strangely enough, the serpent was able to talk Eve into the distorted idea that she didn't have enough. That she needed more. That the God she had so enjoyed was really a stingy slave master, who wanted to hold her back and make sure she never enjoyed all that he did.

She fell for the lie, and so did Adam (see Genesis 3). Instead of the upgrade in satisfaction and self-fulfillment that they had been promised, their loss was of phenomenal proportion. I've often wondered what happened when they reached for something more and ate. The moment was cataclysmic. Did the warm breeze stop blowing? Did the birds stop their singing? Was there an eerie quietness that signaled a new and darker day? Did the animals run for cover? Did the flowers droop? I don't know. All I know is that on that day, everything changed. And the stealthy serpent slithered away, leaving the pair not with the promised new and improved life but with regret, shame, alienation, and guilt.

It was a high-stakes gamble, and they lost—everything. In their shame they realized that the openness and uninhibited joy they'd had in each other was now an awkward, look-the-other-way nakedness that they had never noticed before. So they fashioned coverings of fig leaves, which they wore as public demonstrations that something had changed in the Garden. Big time!

I guess God could have washed his hands of it all or pressed the cosmic Delete button and started all over again. But, amazingly, he loved this awkward, fumbling, failing couple who had now made a complete mess of everything.

Genesis tells us that God walked through the Garden calling their names as they hid in the bushes like little kids who had just thrown a baseball through the picture window and broken the treasured vase. But he was persistent, and they finally came out of hiding, pointing fingers and making excuses. God would have none of it. He sacrificed an animal to clothe their shame with its covering and announced that life would never again be the same for them—or for anyone or anything else, for that matter. Then he expelled them from the Garden, erased their access code, and put angels with flaming swords at the entrance to ensure that they didn't ever try to gain reentry. But he wasn't trying to get even. The Tree of Life was still standing in the Garden, and God knew that if they ate of it, they would live forever in their twisted condition. His love for them couldn't stand the thought.

He had a better, more redemptive plan. Before the eviction notice, he gave them a promise. He promised that someday from the offspring of woman there would be born a victor, a champion, who would crush the head of the destroyer (see Genesis 3:15). And, as Scripture later would affirm, not only would he restore fallen people to God, but the whole creation would be recast into an eternal Eden, locked into righteousness without the possibility of failure or a repeat of the fall . . . forever! A "new heaven and a new earth," as Scripture exclaims (see Revelation 21:1). Where "God himself will be with them as their God. He will wipe away every tear from their eyes, and death shall be no more, neither shall there be mourning, nor crying, nor pain anymore. . . . And he who was seated on the throne said, 'Behold, I am making all things new'" (Revelation 21:3-5). Eden will be restored!

But we're not there yet.

THE RESCUE

Between Eden destroyed and Eden restored, God has been working his redemptive plan to rescue the lost. Throughout history he has been gathering a people for himself. And as he gathers them, he forms them into nations. First the nation of Israel, and second the eternal nation, his church, which Peter calls "a holy nation" (1 Peter 2:9).

The first nation was comprised of a particular people, the Jews. It was the assignment of this nation to show the other nations God's glory and to safely steward the seed of the Messiah, the promised victor, to his birth at just the right time. As Paul tells the Galatians, "When the fullness of time had come, God sent forth his Son, born of woman" (Galatians 4:4).

Unlike the first nation, this second nation is eternal. And right now as you are reading this book, the Jesus Nation is gathering people from every tribe and tongue as it makes its way to Eden restored. Jesus is the King, and we his followers are his nation—a journeying nation that is designed to display the power of Jesus' victory over sin, death, and hell in real space and time. We live to experience and express the revolutionary difference that the ways of Jesus make in our lives.

When we understand what it means to belong to his nation and to become what he intends us to become, we will no longer need to be bewildered with life on this island.

Part 2

BELONGING TO HIS NATION

◆

LIFE WITH JESUS AS KING

Chapter 7

THE BIRTH OF THE NATION

IT MUST HAVE BEEN a great day in Boston. Boxes of British tea were going overboard! The colonists had had it right up to their muskets with the stiffs in London. They were fed up with being treated like they were mere ne'er-do-wells, being charged outrageous taxes as though they were no more than ATMs for the empire. For all they cared, George III could have his tea and keep his pinkie in the air. They were going to take matters into their own hands! So a bunch of scruffy colonists took to the streets, crying, "Give me liberty or give me death," and a new nation was on the verge of being born.

Guys like Peter and John weren't so fortunate. They were up against a wantonly pagan empire that would have snuffed out the likes of them if they had tried anything like the tea-in-the-harbor trick. Rome was unchallenged with the entire known world under its tyrannical thumb. To make matters worse, the Jewish religious leaders were in cahoots with Rome, and their ruthless leader, Herod, got his paycheck from Rome. A once-proud Jewish nation was now an oppressed and marginalized people in the grip of an emperor whose power struck terror in their hearts.

Peter and John were mere fishermen. No vote. No power. No future. Just fish, pay your taxes, and keep your mouth shut! Being Jewish was not cool anymore. But every Jew worth his Torah knew God had promised that the day would come when a Messiah would arrive and deliver them from oppression and restore Israel to its former glory. Prophets had been keeping Jews propped up with this promise for centuries, but nothing ever happened.

Every day was just another day for despairing Jews. Catch more fish. Pay more taxes. Go to the marketplace. Go to church on Saturdays. Raise a family. Spend countless hours talking about what a rotten thing it is to be under the Romans. Be disappointed again and again when wackos come along promising to be messianic, only to get murdered by Rome for being insurrectionists. Get old. Die. That was about it if you were Jewish.

But yet, even in the midst of their humdrum lives, the hope still burned in their souls that someday the real Messiah would come. That he would be the one to overpower the evil grip of Rome, set his people free, and restore the nation Israel to all its past glory!

It was that dream that compelled fishermen, tax collectors, doctors, rich and poor, men and women alike to gamble their lives against the hope that Jesus was the real deal. The fact that they would leave everything for him tells you both how desperate they were for change and how compelling Jesus is when you meet him face-to-face.

And they weren't disappointed . . . at least, not right away.

What a trip. They must have been beside themselves as Jesus constantly got the upper hand when religious guys with their tunics in a twist tried to trap him with their lame questions. Or, think of the jaw-dropping experience of seeing him feed five thousand men and their wives and kids from a meager lunch, brought by a boy who had brown-bagged it to a revival service. Blind people saw! Disabled people walked! Dead people lived! His words flattened raging seas, and his teaching was intriguingly wonderful, authoritative, and true.

And Jesus cared for them. He was so unlike any other leader they had ever known. He really acted like he was there to bless them and not to wield his power and position to use them just to bless himself. Others mattered to him. Regardless! No one escaped the embrace of his mercy and concern. Not prostitutes, not children, not tax collectors, not well-meaning Pharisees, not losers, not winners. Not anyone.

The longer it went on, the more convinced they were that he was indeed the one to restore Israel to its former glory. He would be the king. And they—what a motivating thought—would be his cabinet! In fact, they were so sure of the final outcome that they often argued about who would be the greatest in the coming kingdom. It was such a coveted pursuit that James and John went to the extent of bringing their mother to ask Jesus to make her boys the big shots when he brought the kingdom in. Talk about lowballing!

For sure Judas believed that Jesus would live up to his messianic potential. Judas was in it for the money. He was the treasurer. No doubt he had in mind that he would be the keeper of the till when the kingdom came. So, since he had already been embezzling from what little they had (see John 12:6), he thought he'd soon be into the big bucks when Jesus pulled off his coup.

But the coup would not take place, at least not like the disciples expected. So Judas went off, getting at least thirty pieces of silver to make up for his loss. And the rest of them were left in frightful despair. Jesus was headed to a crucifixion, exactly where the other would-be messiahs had ended up. Though no one had been quite like Jesus, he had still ended up in the same place as the rest of them. And their followers were usually arrested for being coconspirators in the plot to overthrow Rome.

They had gambled and lost. He wouldn't be king, and they wouldn't be big shots after all. Israel was destined to remain a remote, insignificant Roman colony in the vast stretch of the empire. And the disciples would have to reinvent themselves . . . if, that is, they could escape Rome's reach, since they would now be viewed as co-insurrectionists.

But, like so many of us, they had completely misunderstood who Jesus really was and what he was doing on this planet.

Overthrowing Rome would simply have been cosmetic, a waste of Jesus' time. The real problem on planet earth was not Rome . . . or Democrats or Republicans, for that matter. It isn't Hollywood, Hugh Hefner, rapsters, or atheists. It's Satan and all his hellish schemes. Rome was only an expression of the kind of godless rule that is fired up in the boiler room of hell. If it hadn't been Rome messing up people's lives, it would have been something else. Even the nation of Israel had proved that God's people, left to rule themselves, were nothing more than a spiritual and political train wreck looking for a place to happen. And now, if the disciples had their way, they would soon have a crack at running the kingdom of Israel. Deliver us! Think of the mess that the nation would have on its hands if it was run by the likes of pre-Holy-Spirit-filled Peter, power-hungry James and John, and sticky-fingered Judas.

Thankfully, Jesus had something far better in mind. He wasn't about to waste his time going after the cronies of Beelzebub who squatted on their thrones in Rome and Jerusalem. The only way to set things straight was to go after the devil and his demons, who started it all in the first place. Only then could a new nation arise that would be free of the tangling web of hellish impulses. Only then could the liberating ways of a victorious Jesus be planted in good and noble hearts. Only then could a new nation be born that would be eternally about the mission of restoring men and women to their intended purpose: living no longer for themselves but for the honor of proclaiming his excellencies for the glory of God and the pleasure of enjoying him forever!

Three days after his apparent defeat at the hands of Satan, the celebration in the banquet halls of hell came abruptly to a halt as the definitive sounds of victory rang through an empty tomb, making Sunday morning something it had never been before. Independence Day—eternity's Fourth of July! Because it was in those early morning hours that a new nation was born. An eternal nation. A holy nation. A nation in which Jesus is King and to which we, through the finished work on the Cross and the reality of the empty tomb, are privileged to belong.

Understanding who our King really is will make his nation all the more compelling. But the challenge will be to sort through the theories and perceptions that surround the historic Jesus so that we can see him more clearly and follow him more eagerly.

Chapter 8

WILL THE REAL JESUS PLEASE STAND UP?

I HAD ORIGINALLY THOUGHT that I would call this book *Cracking the Jesus Code*. That kind of title seemed to fit into the furor over recent assaults on the historicity and authenticity of Jesus by books like *The Da Vinci Code* and the recent discovery of the ancient manuscripts of the Gospel of Judas. But books shouldn't begin with an apology, and I knew I would have to apologize for a title like that.

The apology would have looked like this: "I'm sorry, but Jesus doesn't have a code that needs to be cracked. He's right out there for all to see!"

NO CODE TO CRACK

Jesus is refreshingly up-front about who he is and why he made the intergalactic trip from the far reaches of eternity to our time-bound, wrong-side-up, fallen outpost. In fact, it was his clarity and candor about his identity that got him into so much trouble back then, and it's the reason why there is so much resistance to him today.

Why we fog up the clarity, I don't know. For some reason, we like to cloak Jesus in a shroud of mystery, and then play Clue with him to see who can come up with the smartest story line. Massive amounts of money have been made in the Who Can Find the Real Jesus game. From the Broadway musical *Jesus Christ Superstar* to Martin Scorsese's controversial movie *The Last Temptation of Christ,* there have been many tales spun about the supposed mystery of the Messiah and his true identity. Books like *The Passover Plot* and Dan Brown's *The Da Vinci Code* have dominated best-seller lists for months on end. The Gospel of Judas recently got prime-time exposure after National Geographic spent millions of dollars to resurrect the account of how Judas and Jesus had actually been coconspirators in an intriguing plot. Adding sizzle to the plot are common themes about Jesus wanting to sleep with Mary Magdalene, the converted prostitute, or his actually doing so. Regular attempts are made to make him a mere mortal, taking him down a notch or two from his claim to be God.

Even religious scholars have gotten into the game. The well-known Jesus Seminar has for the last two decades invited over two hundred religious scholars to bring to the table everything they have found out about Jesus, including their personal, highly researched opinions about what he really said, whether he ever was, or who he really is. All the data is then compiled, and they actually vote on which aspects of their assumptions they think are true by dropping different-colored balls into jars. The different-colored balls are counted and weighed in terms of significance. The conclusion about Jesus is then announced . . . "Red balls have it! Jesus is not all that he's cracked up to be!"

Actually, if I were God—and I know a lot of people, including my wife, are deeply grateful that I am not—I might very well have planned a stealth arrival to our planet to keep people guessing about who I really was. Think of how cool it would have been for God to be here and for no one to know that it was actually him. Hiding his red SuperGod shirt under a white robe, with the old sunglasses, fake nose, and mustache trick, he could sneak into a lot of places without being noticed. Checking up on religious folks to see what they were really like when they thought he wasn't looking would be almost too tantalizing to refuse. He could do the Santa routine, making a list and checking it twice. To most people, that would make a lot of sense, since masses of us assume that God considers it great sport to spend his time finding out who's naughty and nice.

Then, after getting all the scoop, he could quietly disappear. None of this public execution and resurrection fuss to draw attention to his exit—leaving us to the fun and profit of writing our books, filming our movies, and holding high-level seminars to try to figure out if he had really come or who he really had been.

But you've got to give God a lot of credit. He resisted the temptation and arrived on our planet in the person of an unenshrouded, wide-open Jesus. And most surprising, he didn't come to find out who is naughty and nice—he already knows that—he came to shock us about God! To prove once and for all that God is not the stingy, hand-wringing, grimacing, out-of-touch-with-reality god who can't wait to pull the trigger. Rather, he's the God who generously disperses the rare items of wisdom, grace, and mercy to all who have at one time or another slipped up. And that's all of us. He's the God whose love is tough enough to risk a life-threatening rescue mission, so that all of us might recover and experience the ultimate satisfaction that he promises—guaranteed.

So . . . there's really no code to crack.

Unless, that is, it's the code that keeps our hearts at a distance with self-inflicted wounds of doubt and resistance concerning his real mission in our world: to rescue us from ourselves and infuse our lives with hope and purpose.

Not having a code to crack may wreck all the fun for the Jesus-chasers who have made a lot of money telling us what they think he is like. But for the masses in Jesus' day, the reality of his unmasked words, love, and power was profound!

And it must be admitted as an important chunk of evidence that masses in our day have found the real Jesus to be anything but elusive; in fact, they have found him wonderfully candid. And, for the suspicious among us, it is not just the feeble and weak who flee to him for rest and comfort. Though he gladly grants rest and comfort to those who find themselves shoved to the bottom of the heap, the fact is that many highly placed, intelligent, prosperous, and privileged people have found in the midst of their abundance and access to thrills that they are still hanging out the vacancy sign on the door of their hearts. It is these people who are finding that Jesus has come to do exactly what he says he will—cancel the smoke-and-mirrors show and fill the hollow recesses of life with hope and purpose.

Paul Simon sings about what a vacant heart feels like in his song *American Tune*:

> *I don't know a soul who's not been battered;*
> *I don't have a friend who feels at ease.*
> *I don't know a dream that's not been shattered*

Or driven to its knees.
Oh, but it's all right, it's all right
For we lived so well so long.
Still, when I think of the road we're traveling on
I can't help it, I wonder what's gone wrong.

Interesting reflections from one who represents the height of this world's definitions of success: lots of money, fame, popularity, multiple sex partners, and piles of possessions. I'm reminded of the candid confession of author Douglas Coupland in his book *Life After God*:

> Now—here is my secret: I tell it to you with an openness of heart that I doubt I shall ever achieve again, so I pray that you are in a quiet room as you hear these words. My secret is that I need God—that I am sick and can no longer make it alone. I need God to help me give, because I no longer seem to be capable of giving; to help me be kind, as I no longer seem capable of kindness; to help me love, as I seem beyond being able to love.[1]

What I'd like to get across to Paul Simon, Douglas Coupland, and anyone else who will listen is that Jesus did not come to play hide-and-seek with us. When we wake up to the certainty that we need him and are empty and vulnerable without him, thank God! He is anything but elusive.

So why do we think that the real Jesus is such a secret? Why do we feel pressed to reinvent him?

Maybe his claims are too radical, too demanding.

One conclusion that the Jesus Seminar came up with is that Jesus probably said only 20 percent of what is recorded by his followers in the Gospels.

What a relief!

If we can delete statements like "take up your cross and follow me" or his talk about being the only way to God, then life is much more comfortable . . . and I'm still in charge! But then, if 80 percent of what he is reported to have said was made up by the disciples who wrote it for their contemporaries to read, there must have been a lot of readers wagging their heads in disbelief as they said to each other, "He said what? In all the times I was with him, I never heard Jesus say anything like that. These guys are great at storytelling!" To say nothing of the fact that most of the authors died as martyrs because they knew that all they had written about Jesus and his teaching was true; which is why they had embraced every life-transforming, heaven-promising word of it. It's been a long time since anyone died a torturous death to support a story they made up.

Or maybe we can't bring ourselves to embrace Jesus because some of the followers of Jesus we know today are not all that swift. Like Bible bureaucrats, some Jesus people walk around with a sense of superiority, even though there is little resemblance in their lives to the Jesus they claim as their leader. These are religious rule keepers who watch to see if other rule keepers are slipping up and who live to point the finger at non-rule keepers. So it's no surprise that the Jesus most people would like to discover is something different than what the imposters offer us. The retro-regressive attitudes and behavior of some church people would make anyone want something different.

But here's the good news: If you truly find Jesus—the real, uncoded Jesus—he will be wonderfully different from anyone else you have ever met or known. Especially if you grew up in Church World.

My early impressions of Jesus were shaped by the visual images that hung on church walls and the long-white-robed portrayals of him on flannelgraph boards, where figures were stuck to a flannel backdrop with scenery painted on it as the stories of Jesus were told by the teacher. That's probably more information than you needed or wanted . . . sorry . . . but those early experiences are stuck in the recesses of my brain. Consistently Jesus was portrayed as meek, mild, soft, kind, and deferential. Which, to be honest with you, made thoughts of him beating the tar out of the thieves in the Temple seem frightfully inconsistent. And while I'm glad that he is all those things, at the end of the day I'd like him to be a little more compelling than that.

I agree with Mark Driscoll's rebuke of the church for seeing Jesus as a soft-spoken, effeminate, marginalized Galilean hippie. He says he doesn't want a Jesus he could beat up. And while that might be a little raw, I do agree with Mark when he says that we need to see Jesus as the conquering Jesus of Revelation, riding a fiery steed with sword drawn and "King of kings and Lord of lords" tattooed on his thigh.

The Jesus I grew up thinking about was nice, but not very compelling. You'd expect to see him sitting in the front row at church on

Sunday, but you probably wouldn't especially like to play golf with him on Monday.

Thankfully I no longer feel that way. Years ago, I discovered that the code I needed to crack was the code of my misinformed view of him. And as I did, I found that he was still wonderfully nice, but he was undeniably compelling as well. Today I wouldn't play golf with him . . . I'd carry his bag!

Discovering the real Jesus is an adventure of a lifetime, one you'll never tire of. I have found that the longer I live with myself and try to make life all about myself, the more tired I get of myself. But I find Jesus more intriguing, more interesting, more satisfying, more surprising, and more true in his guidance and direction than ever before.

CLUES FROM HIS FOLLOWERS

Step one in the adventure of discovering the real Jesus on your own is to forget what I think about him. I could sit here and pound my fingertips into the keyboard until they were bloody and you were bored to death and went on to more interesting reading. With all due apologies to the Jesus Seminar folk, what they think they know about him and what I know about Jesus on my own is not worth the cost of the print on this page.

But if I had been there, an eyewitness, if I had hung out with him 24/7 for three years, heard him talk about life here and heaven there, experienced his integrity and unusual grip on reality; if I had been stunned in his presence, had listened intently and heard about God and life as I had never heard before, had sensed that his teaching was ringing the lost bells of truth in my heart; if I had seen him make the blind to see, the dead to live; if I had watched him advocate for repentant prostitutes at great risk to himself and his own reputation; if I had witnessed the awkward grimace on the faces of religious folks who tried to trip him up only to discover that Jesus' answers made them look silly. . . . If I had been there all the time, then you should at least give me a shot to tell you what I saw and heard.

In the end, you can reject reports of personal witnesses, or else be convinced. But at least you could say you gave it a shot.

So let's let those who knew him best introduce us to the Jesus they discovered and interestingly enough found to be so right on that they not only gave their lives to telling everyone they could about him but died martyr deaths for him as well. Which, as I have already said, is pretty solid evidence that there may be something more to Jesus than meets the let's-vote-on-Jesus eye.

But before you write off people like Matthew, John, Peter, and the rest of them as saints posing for medieval art, a brief profile of the kind of people they were is going to be interesting. And I think the fact that these kinds of individuals followed him will show that Jesus is truly compelling.

A group of them were seasoned, rugged fishermen. If we could put it in today's terms, they were the kind of guys who could be found early in the morning at Sarah's Seaside Twenty-Four-Hour Café, downing their bagels and lox over coffee before hitting the sea. With well-worn caps tipped back on their heads showing the tan lines across their foreheads and fading tattoos on their biceps, these no-nonsense, street-smart kind of guys had a healthy skepticism for people in power and didn't swallow every hook, line, and sinker that was thrown their way. As they jammed their cigarette butts into the ashtray and called to Sarah for another bagel, they were trashing Rome and damning the treacherous ways of Caesar and his minion, Herod. But, these were the kind of guys who left the fishing business to follow Jesus . . . and though sometimes faltering and second-guessing, never turned back.

And it wasn't just fishermen. Take Matthew, the savvy businessman who was so into money and success that he sold out to the oppressive regime of Rome to collect their exorbitant taxes from his own country-men. Worse yet, he, along with all other tax collectors (Zacchaeus types), was fond of adding a few assessments of his own to line his pockets. This was the kind of guy who didn't care what anyone thought of him, as long as the revenue stream was flowing. He left his lucrative career to follow Jesus.

This makes for an interesting contrast to Simon the Zealot. Simon got his nickname from his association with the resistance force dedicated to overthrowing the tyranny of Rome. He no doubt would spill his own blood in the streets—or the blood of others, if necessary—to get the job done. He was like a militiaman who keeps Uzis in his garage and who protests by not paying taxes—which would have been a huge problem to Matthew, not to mention how Simon would have felt in return.

Yet polar opposites like these riveted their lives to Jesus. Rising above their preferences and political points of view, they became proud members of the Jesus Nation and refused to let the lesser issues of life distract them.

The point is that these guys weren't losers looking for a free lunch.

And I need to add that it wasn't just the men. From hookers to homemakers, women followed him, adoringly worshiped him, and felt safe with him.

These were real people, of the "a lot like us" variety.

And they were there.

They had a closer look than anyone else. They saw him in private and they saw him in public. Every move was calibrated by the haunting thought that they had given up everything to follow him. And, after three years of constant exposure, they were not disappointed. In fact, after he left they just kept talking about him and welcomed others to know the solid joy of knowing what they knew. Since then multiple millions have listened and believed and multiple millions have not been disappointed.

But we should be prepared at the beginning of this discovery. What these people have to tell us is often an expectation-shattering surprise. It was for them, and it is for us. And the greatest surprise of all is that Jesus' revolution not only brought an answer to the weirdness of life as we know it but also established a nation that gives all who join it a new sense of purpose and life-rearranging identity.

Chapter 9

LIFE ON PURPOSE

IF YOU HAVE TRAVELED IN EUROPE, you realize that by comparison, we have no history in America. In fact, you realize that, at best, we're the new kids on the block when it comes to ancient legacies. Martie and I love the English countryside. One of our favorite towns in rural England has a church where God has been worshiped since the 1300s. Other churches and buildings go further back than that. But if you are British, French, or German and start feeling prideful about your history, take note. A quick mention of Chinese history, with sophisticated dynasties that date back thousands of years before the birth of Jesus, will put anyone else's history into even better perspective. Anyone for trying to build the Great Wall of China without modern technology?

But if you are talking about the Jesus Nation, there is no history that rivals its legacy. Its foundations were laid in eternity past, by none other than the three members of the Trinity; it was predicted soon after the Creation; it was announced by the prophets; and it has been sweeping the globe with its revolutionary, life-transforming power since the time of Christ's birth over two thousand years ago. It has been led by some of the most familiar names in history, to say nothing of the fact that its ultimate hero, Jesus, has a worldwide, unrivaled reputation that remains strong to this day.

And while all earthly nations come and go and leave in their wake legacies for historians to spin, the Jesus Nation is compellingly different. It's eternal, for one thing. It's happily multicultural, optimistic, undaunted, and victorious. When the greatest of nations are no more, the Jesus Nation will be in full force.

People who belong to the Jesus Nation are dynamically different, as well. They live, think, and act differently, and they have a clear and compelling purpose in life. Jesus Nationals don't just read headlines and watch from a distance as their nation rises and falls in the currents of global economies and politics. They are personally involved and responsible in carrying out clearly prescribed duties that move the national agenda forward. They are motivated by the fact that they are a part of a significant movement that is worth sacrificing for and surrendering to. They know who they are, where they are going, and what they are supposed to do. And when the going gets tough, they don't give up, because they know that this is not the only world they have—their nation is on a journey to a better world that is yet to come. And best of all, they have a ruler who loves and cares for them and a ruler that they love and trust implicitly. That in and of itself makes belonging to this nation really unique.

So, let's unwrap the Jesus Nation and get a grip on what it means to belong.

TRANSFERRED TO THE KINGDOM

Throughout the ministry of Jesus and in the writing of the apostles, there is much discussion about the Kingdom of God, sometimes called the Kingdom of Heaven. And these Kingdom references, while sometimes veiled in parabolic language and couched in theological thought, are in the end intensely personal. For instance, Paul tells us that we have been transferred (literally, "uprooted" or "transplanted") from the domain of darkness into the Kingdom of God's beloved Son (see Colossians 1:13). And when Jesus said that the "kingdom of God is at hand" (Mark 1:15) and when he prayed that the Kingdom would come "on earth as it is in heaven" (Matthew 6:10), he meant that it was his intention that the eternal Kingdom would begin to emerge now through us, his followers.

John G. Stackhouse rightly indicates how that takes place when he writes that the Kingdom of God began to take form when "Jesus' life inaugurated God's direct and uncompromised rule on earth. The Kingdom of God is where, we might say, God's ways are the way, and God's rules are the rules. . . . The Kingdom of God is thus where God's authority is joyfully embraced as legitimate and welcome."[1] Living out his rule and demonstrating his ways as we joyfully embrace his authority in our lives is the part we play in the Kingdom's becoming real and present in our world. This present world will never experience the full manifestation of the ultimate and eternal Kingdom where Jesus reigns in totality, but it can be expressed and seen through our lives. This is what *belonging* to the Jesus Nation and *becoming* an active participant in his Kingdom means.

Being a part of his nation, the Kingdom of God, means that we are a part of something bigger than ourselves, that we are not alone in some individualistic religious pursuit. It means that we belong to a diverse cultural kaleidoscope of people from every tribe and nation, that we all share the same identity and are following the same hero. We courageously live to support each other in the face of forces that are far stronger than the strongest of us yet are already defeated for us. It means that his ways are our ways and that his rule is readily welcomed in our heads and hearts. The result is that we will live and act differently, as our hero Jesus is different, in sometimes radical and revolutionary ways. Because living out our belonging to the Jesus Nation is not just something we do: It is our identity; it is who we are. For us not to live as followers of the King is to fail to live up to who we really are.

OUR KINGDOM: THE NATION

When Scripture talks about us belonging to the "Kingdom of God," it is much like belonging to, let's say, the Cubs Nation. I wince when I write that, but we need help to understand what may be the most revolutionary concept that God ever tried to communicate to us. Belonging to the Kingdom of God and becoming all we need to become as Kingdom citizens is a central theme of the New Testament and obviously far more important than anything that has to do with baseball or any other treasured experience on this planet. In fact, it's more important every day of my life!

The term *kingdom*, while very expressive in nondemocratic societies where there are kings, queens, and subjects, doesn't carry a lot of weight for those of us who live in democracies and only encounter kingdoms in storybooks and cartoons. And while clearly there are some deep and important theological connotations to the concept of a kingdom—for instance, we don't get to vote, and we have a king whose words and ways are always wonderfully right—it remains a foreign notion. But we are familiar with what it means to live in a nation.

Let me hasten to say that I'm not interested in rewriting Scripture. Kingdom, clearly understood, is a precise picture of what Jesus means when he calls us to belong to him and to become an active participant in his enterprise. But it's important to note that Scripture references the term *nation* as well. In fact, the concept of God's using a nation of people to show the world a preview of the ways and the rule of his Kingdom is an important theme in both the Old and New Testaments.

GOD'S PLAN FOR THE NATIONS

The very first nation emerged out of God's plan to keep his promise that from the seed of woman an ultimate conqueror would come (see Genesis 3:15). But on the heels of that promise, things were looking grim. If all you read of Genesis after the Fall is the next chapter, you wonder whether or not the slippery serpent had pulled off a stunning coup. The first righteous seed of woman, Abel, was killed by his brother, Cain. Now, who would be left to fulfill the promise? As far as Satan knew, Abel was the promised champion who would deal him the promised deathblow. Did he think he had averted the plan? Then Cain spawned a sophisticated yet violently murderous culture that was filled with pride and self-glorification (see Genesis 4:17-24).

But just when it seemed that the whole world was headed for the dump, a glimmer of hope appeared. Seth was born and, as Genesis 4:26 says, mankind began to call on the name of the Lord. Then a line of godly individuals to carry out God's plan emerged. First there was Enoch, then Noah, and then Abraham. With the arrival of Abraham on the scene, God began articulating his plan to birth a nation, through whom he would carry out his loving and redemptive purposes. Genesis 12:2 records God saying to Abraham (then called Abram), "I will make of you a great nation." Already there were multiple nations on the earth. But the purpose of this nation was to bring the Messiah seed to fruition. And the success of this nation would be a worthy enterprise, since God promised Abraham, "In you all the families of the earth shall be blessed" (Genesis 12:3).

The promise began to take shape when Abraham's miracle baby, Isaac, was born. Isaac's son Jacob would later be named Israel—the nation's namesake. Israel's sons would establish the twelve tribes that would comprise the distinctive clans in this original nation of God. Israel would now begin the three-thousand-year trek to Bethlehem, where the ultimate nation would be born in the person of Jesus, who "in the fullness of time" was born of a virgin and would live for thirty-three years to show us how to live in his nation. And it is this Jesus who, through his death and resurrection, would inaugurate his eternal nation. A nation over which he would eternally rule in righteousness, justice, and peace.

It is exactly this thought that Peter had in mind when he reminded us that we are "a holy nation, a people for his own possession, that you may proclaim the excellencies of him who called you out of darkness into his marvelous light. Once you were not a people, but now you are God's people" (1 Peter 2:9-10).

So we need to put away any notion that because we are a "New Testament kind of person" we don't belong to a nation, or to a kingdom, if you prefer. It's clear from Peter's words that being a part of this "holy nation" is our central identity. The name of a country stamped on the cover of your passport may indicate that you are a citizen of that nation, but that's not your true identity if you are a follower of Jesus. Your country is merely the place where you live. In fact, it's the place where you live out the dynamics of your true nationality as a follower of Christ.

Peter helps us to understand what this means by describing the nature and life-transforming dynamics of the Jesus Nation. So, listening closely to Peter in this context is important if we are going to get a grip on our national identity. According to Peter, belonging to this holy nation has three pivotal implications for our lives, implications that cancel our *bewilderment* with the frantic futility of life as we know it by articulating the distinctiveness of life in his nation.

Peter identifies these three distinctives that mark the lives of authentic Jesus nationals. First, life is no longer about me. Jesus is preeminent! Second, we are a holy nation living differently, as Jesus is different. And third, it is the excellence of this different life that catches the attention of and gives us credibility in a sometimes hostile and resistant world. Understanding these dynamics and applying them to our lives is what the next three chapters are about.

Chapter 10

WHO'S NUMBER ONE?

ONE OF MY ALL-TIME FAVORITE memories about our kids is the time when my seven-year-old daughter Libby asked, "Daddy, are we famous?" My immediate response was, "No, Libby, we're not famous." She thought about it for a second and indignantly said, "Well, we would be if more people knew about us!"

Poor Libby, only seven and already wondering about herself—whether people liked us or whether a lot of people knew about us! Poor Libby, already tied up in the world of "me"! And, unfortunately, this preoccupation with herself is something she will never grow out of, because we all struggle with the irresistible gravity of "me" and the tendency to live as though life is indeed all about "me"!

But I need to tell you, if life is going to be all about you, then someday you will be bored to tears. If you think that you are cool enough to entertain yourself with yourself for the long haul, you are in for a surprise. I want to be gentle here, but none of us are special enough to enthrall ourselves with ourselves for the rest of our lives!

I'm now in my sixties, and as I mentioned earlier I have to admit that I'm already getting tired of *me*. I am tired of trying to deal with the insecurities that have haunted me for years. Tired of the failures in my life that I think I have finally gotten victory over just to have them pop up again. Tired of the carnal way I feel when people talk about their favorite preacher and it's not me! Tired of looking in the rearview mirror and wishing I had done things differently. Tired of the awkward way I feel on those rare occasions when people praise me. I am just flat-out getting tired of me.

But, after sixty years, I have to say, I'm still not tired of Jesus. I never get tired of praising him and hearing him praised. I still stand amazed at the unusual grace and mercy that he continues to pour out on me daily. As life goes on, I find Jesus to be more adventuresome, interesting, challenging, fresh, and compelling than ever before. I continue to find him wonderfully different—anything but boring! No wonder Paul said that he counted even the best things about himself like dung compared to the surpassing value of getting to know Jesus (see Philippians 3:7-8, KJV).

When you're young, you think you'll live forever. But when you get to be my age, you can see your mortality approaching on the horizon. If you're in my age bracket, it's not difficult to see yourself someday sitting alone in the corner of a room at the nursing home waiting for the lunch bell to ring. And if life has been all about you, that's going to be a really bad day—because there's nothing left of you that's worth getting excited about! But if your life has been all about Jesus, it will be a really good day—because Jesus will be just as wonderful as he has ever been. And you might just hear him whisper in your heart, "You're almost home!"

THE CENTRALITY OF JESUS

What I like about the Jesus Nation is that it's all about him.

I'm struck by the fact that immediately after Paul tells us we have been transplanted into the Kingdom of Jesus, he reminds us about the "number-oneness" of Jesus over all things. He writes:

> He is the image of the invisible God, the firstborn of all creation. For by him all things were created, in heaven and on earth, visible and invisible, whether thrones or dominions or rulers or authorities—all things were created through him and for him. And he is before all things, and in him all things hold together. And he is the head of the body, the church. He is the beginning, the firstborn from the dead, that in everything he might be preeminent. (Colossians 1:15-18)

That settles the issue. And since he is number one in everything, nobody gets a pass on this. Frankly, after I read the list of his credentials, it seems like a really bad idea to try to one-up him with my own ideas and plans.

So it should not come as a surprise to us that, before the apostle Peter rolls out the idea that we are a holy nation, he also establishes the centrality and rightful authority of Jesus in all of life, work, and worship (1 Peter 2:4-9). He begins by quoting from the Old Testament prophet Isaiah (see 28:16), who spoke on behalf of God when he predicted the coming of Christ, saying, "Behold, I am laying in Zion a stone, a cornerstone chosen and precious, and whoever believes in him will not be put to shame" (1 Peter 2:6). Peter continues, "The honor is for you who believe, but for those who do not believe"—and here he quotes Psalm 118:22 and Isaiah 8:14—"'The stone that the builders rejected has become the cornerstone . . . a stone of stumbling, and a rock of offense.'" Peter concludes, "They stumble because they disobey the word, as they were destined to do" (1 Peter 2:7-8).

What Peter is saying is foundational to our understanding of what it means for us to bow to the preeminence of Jesus.

First, when our lives reflect our commitment to the preeminence of Jesus, we find our significance in the honor of being a part of his plan, rather than in our own plans and successes.
Peter reminds us that God has assigned Jesus to accomplish the most important enterprise in the history of our universe, the redemption of mankind and our eternal restoration to him. So at the very top, to be a part of the Jesus Nation means that we have been called to participate in a God-designed plan in which Jesus is preeminent. The most important plan ever.

That's no small thing!

Regardless of who you are or who you aren't, winner or loser, you are a recipient of and a participant in history's greatest event. It's far bigger than you, and thankfully it's not about you . . . although the benefits for you are out of this world. But then, life is always better when you are involved in something that is bigger and better than you are. If it's always about "me" and my limited perspectives and agendas, then at best I'll be living my life for all the lesser, comparatively insignificant and misguided plans that I dream up for myself. No wonder Peter calls it an honor for those who believe. Jesus is the undisputed, unrivaled redeemer, and there is an overwhelming sense of privilege and significance in being chosen to be a part of the most important enterprise in all of history.

Second, the reality that Jesus is central means that we no longer need to keep driving our lives into the abutments of our own foolish mistakes.
The imagery that Peter uses reflects the fact that in Jesus we have a clear sense of direction in life.

There is a world of meaning in the fact that Jesus is called the *cornerstone.* Immediately, I think of that last limestone block that we put into the corner of a new building with a date on it and a bunch of memorabilia stuffed behind. But we can't read this verse with that picture in mind. In ancient times, the cornerstone was the most important building block that was laid. It was a huge stone, the first to be laid at the corner of the footprint of the soon-to-be-constructed building. It was placed carefully by the master builder, and all the building and its construction were measured off the stone. In fact, the cornerstone defined the shape and design of the structure.

This is a life-changing concept. Jesus defines all that we are and all that we are becoming. His will, ways, wisdom, mission, and passions drive and define all that we are and do. To live in the nation where Jesus is preeminent means that someone who is far smarter than we are is driving the bus of our lives.

I have the privilege of serving at Cornerstone University in Grand Rapids, Michigan. I love the name of our university! It gives us a clear sense of who we are. All we do is defined by Jesus—by his wisdom in all of our academics, by his will in all of our planning, by his ways in all of our actions, by his mission in terms of sending our grads out to influence our world for him, and by his passion to do all we do to bring glory to the Father. In the process of building lives that matter, we are seeking to build an on-campus model of what living in the Jesus Nation looks like. But this should be happening everywhere the name of Jesus is proclaimed—not just on a college campus but also in our homes, our churches, our neighborhoods, where we work, and in any sphere where we have influence.

So, if you have been delivered from the domain of darkness and planted into the nation of God's beloved Son, you no longer need to experiment with how you will live your life. Jesus does that for us. He's our cornerstone, and as such he drives and defines all we do.

And, we should note, he is the *chief* cornerstone! No one trumps him. He's the man.

When he drives and defines our lives, we are liberated from the silly mistakes that we keep making over and over again in our relationships, bank accounts, credit card exchanges; with our enemies; in our attitudes and twisted actions. And, with his will and wisdom shaping our lives, we are never bewildered about what life really is all about. Every decision has meaning, and every pursuit has a worthwhile ring to it. We never feel empty at the end, and our sense of meaning and purpose is large and satisfying.

Third, when Jesus is preeminent, we will have an unshakable confidence that his plans, his ways, and his wisdom will never disappoint us.
This means that we no longer need to place our hope and trust in the smoke and mirrors of our own desires and dreams. Jesus' desires for us are perfect, and we can be certain that he is able to finish the victory that he has begun on our behalf. When Peter says that those of us who believe in Jesus will not be put to shame, he is reminding us that we will never be ashamed of casting our lot with him.

It's easy to feel that we have sided with a losing cause when evil seems to triumph, when we are marginalized, mocked, or ridiculed for following him. You can feel like a loser pretty quickly when everyone around you cheats through life and prospers, while you do what's right and end up with the short end of the stick. But every time I'm tempted to think that I have given my life to a losing cause, I remember the ringing affirmation of Jesus' ultimate victory in Philippians 2:9-11: "Therefore God has highly exalted him and bestowed on him the name that is above every name, so that at the name of Jesus every knee should bow, in heaven and on earth and under the earth, and every tongue confess that Jesus Christ is Lord, to the glory of God the Father."

Life is a full-length feature film. If you simply take one of the frames and freeze it, you can get a pretty bleak view of staying faithful to Jesus and start to doubt his faithfulness to you. But you can't freeze-frame life. You have to let the film run to its conclusion. On that day, Jesus wins! And if Jesus wins, so do you. As for me, the only shame I could feel on that day would be that of knowing I had bailed on him because I thought he was a losing cause.

Peter is assuring us that Jesus will not disappoint us. Not ultimately. After so many years of following and trusting him, I can attest that the

Lord has never disappointed me. Throughout life I have had friends disappoint me; colleagues have not kept their word; politicians, the Cubs, and a host of others have let me down. To be honest, I have disappointed myself on more occasions than I would like to admit. But Jesus has always been there as a faithful and true friend. Now, there have been times when I have felt that he has disappointed me, only to find in time that what I thought was a disappointment was actually his *appointment* to do something important in my life that couldn't have been done any other way.

When you have crowned yourself as the central feature of your life, only to end up thinking that something is wrong with life—or, worse, that something is wrong with you—remember who the preeminent person of the nation is. As the most important one, he gives what you can't give yourself—in fact, what no one else can give you. He gives true significance, clear and wise direction, and something solidly, ultimately reliable to lean on.

In my book *Simply Jesus and You,* I tell the story of being seated at a dinner next to Billy Graham. The meal was just about finished when I asked Dr. Graham the question I had hoped to ask him all evening. Billy, eighty years old at the time, was lucid and interesting. Wondering what he would say about his highest joys in life, I asked, "Of all your experiences in ministry, what have you enjoyed most?"

Then (thinking I might have to help him out a little), I quickly added, "Was it your time spent with presidents and heads of state? Or was it—"? Before I could finish my next sentence, Billy swept his hand across the linen tablecloth, as if to push my lame suggestions onto the floor.

"None of that," he said. "By far the greatest joy of my life has been my fellowship with Jesus. Hearing him speak to me, having him guide me, sensing his presence with me and his power through me. This has been the highest pleasure of my life!"

It was spontaneous, unscripted, and unrehearsed. There wasn't even a pause.

With a life full of stellar experiences and worldwide fame behind Billy Graham, it was simply Jesus who was on his mind and on his heart. If anyone could be taken with himself, it would be Dr. Graham. But for Billy, Jesus was everything. His lifelong experience with Jesus had made its mark, and Billy was satisfied.

I found Billy Graham's statement that evening to be challenging and convicting. Challenging because I want to be able to say that; convicting because I'm not sure I am there yet. But with everything in me, I want what he has experienced.

It would be easy to think that you'd expect someone like Billy Graham to have that kind of intimacy with Jesus—he's the anointed global evangelist. Easy to think that common, ordinary folk like the rest of us can't expect to get there. So if you're thinking that, let me tell you about my grandmother.

Born of pioneer stock in Michigan, she married a frontier farmer and gave birth to her children in a drafty, second-floor corner bedroom at home. She lived to keep her house for her family and to cook meals for the farmhands, far away from the hustle and bustle of high society. No one but friends and family knew her name. I remember her asking me when I was a boy if I knew what her favorite hymn was. Actually, I did. I had often heard her singing it as she went about the duties of her day. To this day I remember the words:

> I come to the garden alone
> While the dew is still on the roses,
> And the voice I hear falling on my ear
> The Son of God discloses.
> And He walks with me, and He talks with me,
> And He tells me I am His own.
> And the joy we share as we tarry there
> None other has ever known.
> —Charles Austin Miles, "In the Garden"

She shared the same joy in Jesus that Billy had discovered.

And if she can, so can I. So can you.

In his nation, Jesus is the preeminent one, and he is there for us to find our significance in him, our direction for living and our confidence for ultimately never being ashamed or disappointed that we have cast our lot with him. All of this for "the joy we share as we tarry there."

Chapter 11

VIVE LA DIFFÉRENCE

WHEN JESUS IS PREEMINENT, people will see a difference in our lives because Jesus is different. And when we are in the process of becoming different as he is different, we are in the process of becoming holy—or, as Peter puts it, "a holy nation." I can understand why most of us might think that we could never be a part of a holy nation. But before you decide to go back to life on your own terms, let's think through this together. Too often the thought of being holy conjures up mental images of sinless perfection. That would be the end for all of us. But interestingly, God's Word says that "as he who called you is holy, you also be holy in all your conduct, since it is written, 'You shall be holy, for I am holy'" (1 Peter 1:15-16).

Now, if there's anyone who knows that none of us can be perfect, it's God. And yet he requires that we be holy as he is. It's either a cynical setup for failure from a God who enjoys seeing us give it our best and then collapse on the track before the finish line, or else he knows that becoming holy is a distinct possibility. In case you are wondering, it's the latter! So if you have given up on holiness in your life because you are not perfect, then welcome to the joy of what true holiness can really mean in your imperfect life.

If we get past that perfection objection, you may also be put off by thinking that living a holy life means you need to be quiet, passive, reflective, even somber, with hands folded and always thinking sacred thoughts. As if holiness meant you could never stand up and shout in your living room when your team made a dazzling play to win the game in the last few seconds, or throw that sponge brick at your TV set if the ref made a lame call. As if you certainly would never laugh boisterously or pull off a trick on your friend. Guess again.

You can be holy and be cool and be real all at the same time. And as for holiness making you out of touch and irrelevant, actually, holiness puts you in touch with God, who above everything else is intensely relevant. So let's talk about what it means to be holy in a holy nation. The word "holy" in the Hebrew Old Testament is *kadosh*, and in the Greek New Testament it is *hagios*. In both cases the word means different, distinct, separate, set apart, other. God is holy because he is different. Completely different. There is no one or no thing that is like him. Nothing can compare to him. He is totally other. That's why his sinlessness, his perfection, makes him holy. There is no one like that. But he is different in every other way as well. He knows everything; he is transcendent, all-powerful, sovereign. His justice, mercy, love, righteousness, grace, and all other attributes are perfectly blended and flawlessly executed.

So when God separated Israel to be a "holy nation" (Exodus 19:6), he had in mind that Israel would be different from other nations—as their God was different from other nations' gods—and that their lives, worship, and community would reflect that difference. They were God's people, and they needed to be like their God. They would worship the one true God and not be idolatrous. They would not practice the ways of the sexually perverted pagan nations. They would value life, welcome the stranger, feed the poor, and obey their God. And they were to practice purity rituals to reflect the fact that God is pure in every way. In fact, much of what we read in Exodus (the Ten Commandments and other detailed instructions) was meant to set Israel apart—a distinct reflection of the meaning of the word *kadosh*—and to make them a holy nation as God is a holy God. But, knowing that Israel wouldn't ever be able to measure up to him, God set up a whole system of sacrifices, so that they could find forgiveness as a way to get back on track again.

In his book *The Jesus Way*, Eugene Peterson brilliantly traces the distinctiveness of Israel among the nations. He writes,

> Over a period of eighteen hundred years or so, the Hebrews, our ancestor people of God, lived in proximity to a succession of great world civilizations—absolutely stunning civilizations,

extravagantly splendid in architecture and art, masters of all the latest technologies, with military accomplishments that boggle the imagination still, sophisticated organizational and bureaucratic systems capable of directing huge work forces and an international economy, and religious establishments that articulated religious systems capable of integrating entire populations in a common belief and practice. None of these cultures were fly-by-night or flash-in-the-pan. Their influence endured for hundreds, some of them for thousands, of years. . . .

It is one of the wonders of the world that they were not absorbed by the power and beauty and wealth and learning brandished and celebrated by the kings and queens, the generals and priests, the gods and goddesses of those empires. The Hebrews seemed impervious to the whole show. They maintained what was always, given the sociopolitical forces around them, a precarious identity. But maintain it they did.[1]

When Peter speaks of the Kingdom of Jesus Nationals being a holy nation, he has the same thing in mind. Privileged to be living in the most advanced culture in the history of mankind, which is full of dazzling technological marvels, we are to be different. Just as God is different.

If you have been hanging around church for a lot of years, as I have, it's likely you default to the old "I don't drink, dance, smoke, chew, or go with girls who do" way of thinking when trying to pull off the holiness assignment. Well, those kinds of things may separate you from certain aspects of the world, but holiness is not first and foremost separation *from the world.* True holiness is being set apart (*hagios*) *unto God*, becoming like God in the world we live in. It is the character and nature of God that determines our personal holiness agenda. I don't know if God would smoke a cigar, but you can be sure that merely abstaining is not what he had in mind when he called us to be holy.

With that in mind, a lot of the old lists fade into relative obscurity, particularly given the fact that those who lived by such lists were often intolerant, merciless, gossipy, unjust, and a whole bunch of things that were just like our world and not like God at all. Mastering a short, man-made list of things we don't do can make us pretty proud of ourselves and quite set apart from others who aren't like us. And *that* is not like God at all.

And while being holy certainly means that we shun evil, being holy is also about becoming different as God is different in his love, mercy, kindness, justice, patience, integrity, humility—and a compelling list of other aspects of God that we can emulate in our lives. Being holy is living to imitate God's fully faceted goodness. It is an inspiring and invigorating pursuit. In fact, the Old Testament writers are onto this in a major way. In passages such as Psalm 24:3-4, Psalm 15:1-5, and Isaiah 6:5-7 we are called to reflect God's holiness in lives of individual integrity and social justice.

And, knowing that none of us could pull all of this off in sinless perfection, Jesus died for us as the ultimate sacrifice, so that we could be forgiven when we act in unholy ways and get back on track again.

Because we are to be a "holy nation," this compelling and comprehensive call to holiness is a significant part of what it means to belong to the Jesus Nation. Yet, outside of normal church activities, a lot of us who call ourselves Christians aren't all that different from our world at all and in many respects not much like God. We are stingy with our resources; we tend to be unforgiving; we are more prone to be mad instead of merciful, grumpy instead of gracious, indifferent instead of compassionate; in business we tend to care more about profit than people and to be unbothered by the injustices around us—unless, of course, the injustice has been done to us. Again I appreciate Eugene Peterson's perspective:

> My concern is provoked by the observation that so many who
> understand themselves to be followers of Jesus, without hesi-
> tation, and apparently without thinking, embrace the ways
> and means of the culture as they go about their daily living
> "in Jesus' name." But the ways that dominate our culture have
> been developed either in ignorance or in defiance of the ways
> that Jesus uses to lead us as we walk the streets and alleys, hike
> the trails, and drive the roads in this God-created, God-saved,
> God-blessed, God-ruled world in which we find ourselves. They
> seem to suppose that "getting on in the world" means getting
> on in the world on the world's terms, and that the ways of Jesus
> are useful only in a compartmentalized area of life labeled "reli-
> gious." This is wrong thinking, and wrong living. Jesus is an
> alternative to the dominant ways of the world, not a supplement
> to them.[2]

Because Jesus is the fullness of God and exhibits the glory of the only begotten of the Father (see John 1:14, KJV), then following him is indeed the way to holiness.

Martie and I used to spend a few weeks in England each year at a little cottage where I did some studying and writing. We grew to love England, its culture, and its people. Just hearing the British talk was worth the price of the transatlantic ticket. One of the experiences we enjoyed was what Brits call "The Last Night at the Proms." During the summer, all over England, outdoor concerts held on the sloping lawns of ancient estates are called "the proms." On the last scheduled prom of the season, some of England's grand patriotic songs are featured: "Rule, Britannia"; "Land of Hope and Glory"; "God Save the Queen." These and other national favorites are not only performed by a musical group but also sung lustily by the hundreds of British nationals who sit on their blankets with wine, cheese, and wicker picnic baskets. These last nights often include flyovers of vintage WWII aircraft that buzz the crowd at just the right moment. Fireworks provide a sizzling backdrop as the symphony and guest artists passionately stir the hearts of the locals. When the last song is sung, everyone is standing, waving little British flags to a rousing rendition of a patriotic tune.

It's quite captivating. So much so, in fact, that Martie and I got our own little flags and often joined in the celebration as though we were true-blue Brits. It didn't seem like a problem until the summer that we brought a few of our children and their spouses over to visit us. What would a trip to England be like without going to the Last Night at the Proms? They thoroughly enjoyed the evening—until it came time to stand and wave the flags to the tune of the closing anthem. Martie and I stood with great enthusiasm and joined the crowd. Our children were astonished—*aghast* or *ashamed* might be better words. I can still hear them shouting over the music, "Mom, Dad! What are you doing? You're not British. You're Americans!" There we were, lifelong American citizens, caught up in the exuberance of the moment, acting like we were Brits. There was something wrong with the picture!

I sometimes wonder if that's how God feels about us. If he would say, "What are you doing living like that? You belong to my nation!" It's a troubling thought that not many would know we belong to this holy nation, since we just blend in with the locals. Outside of church activities and a few religious rituals that we are bound to, we are not all that different from everyone else. Not really.

In his book *Buck-Naked Faith*, Eric Sandras is a little raw but frightfully honest. He starts off his book by describing a sexual encounter he had during a period in his life in which he was the student leader of a 250-member college ministry:

> Like the token heathens I evangelized, I occasionally wanted to enjoy the benefits of the opposite sex without all the responsibility my faith and morality attached to them. . . .
>
> God had a different agenda that night. He was going to invade my private world and shake it to its core. From this moment on, my soul would be scarred. I would forever know that the painful consequences of duplicity far outweigh its benefits.
>
> The dagger came as I smugly rolled over in bed, feeling pretty good about my performance and slightly enjoying the rush that accompanies risks like I was taking. Then I noticed some tears welling up in the girl's eyes. They weren't tears of joy or even deep hurt; they were tears of disappointment. This became even more evident in the five words that accompanied those drops of disillusionment: "I thought you were different." . . .
>
> Suddenly, I realized that I did indeed know this woman, who hours ago had only been the target of my carnal desires. How could I have been so blind? She had just started attending the weekly campus meetings of our university fellowship. She was simply trying to make sense out of Christianity and religion. In *my* eyes she had only been an object of my attraction, but in *her* eyes I had been Jesus.[3]

You may or may not be sleeping around. But I wonder how many people around your life are saying, "I thought you were different." Let's be honest here. As I noted earlier, if we say that we are followers of Jesus, members of the Jesus Nation, people around us don't expect us to be gossipy, stingy, mad at our enemies (both personal and political), intolerant, quick to pass judgment, dishonest in our business dealings, glancing with long looks at scantily clad members of the opposite sex, unloving, despairing in the midst of difficulty, or a host of other things that we might do to earn those five words. Interesting, isn't it, that while most of the people around us have never read the Bible, they have an instinctive sense of what we should not be like. They expect us to be different, to be like our God in good and meaningful ways.

Making Jesus unconditionally preeminent will make us different. And if we understand the power of that difference, we will say with the French, *Vive la différence!* Because the difference, as Peter reminds us, shows off the excellencies of Jesus.

EXCELLENCE IN LIVING

RUSH LIMBAUGH—whatever you think of him—refers to his nationally syndicated talk show as being on the "EIB network." *EIB* stands for "excellence in broadcasting." When he rolls out the EIB theme, it is always done with a flourish of bravado and pride. If you belong to the Jesus Nation, you could wear a T-shirt with the initials *EIL*—"excellence in living."

For all of us who have been bewildered by a life that has no steady, compelling purpose, welcome to the purpose that belonging to the Jesus Nation provides. Peter links our national holiness to Christ's compelling purpose for our lives, a purpose that can be lived out in any situation of life . . . anytime, anywhere. He writes that we are a "holy nation, a people for his own possession, that you may proclaim the excellencies of him who called you out of darkness into his marvelous light" (1 Peter 2:9).

It is our purpose in life to live distinctively in countercultural ways and, in so doing, to show off the excellencies of Jesus, who has called us out of darkness into his light. No one was more countercultural than Jesus. He came to show us how to live in a whole new way, and that way is excellent. And when we live his way, the world sees the excellent ways of Jesus showing up in our lives.

So what would those *excellencies* look like? The word literally means "eminent qualities." In the plural, it speaks to the essential excellence of God's character expressed through deeds that reveal his character.[1] This means that when you live in ways that reveal the excellence of his character in word and deed, you are fulfilling the purpose of belonging to the Jesus Nation.

When you love unconditionally . . . When you care for the poor, marginalized, and oppressed . . . When you show mercy to the guilty and grace to the undeserving . . . When you forgive the cruelest of offenses . . . When you are generous in spirit and resources . . . When you are content . . . When you express integrity, humility, and honesty . . . When people matter most to you . . . When you activate the goodness of God in ways that make the invisible God visible through your actions and attitudes wherever, whatever, and with whomever, you are living a purposeful and productive life . . . the life you are intended to live as a Jesus National.

What fascinates me is Peter's point that, in a hostile and resistant culture, the key to our prevailing victory is living out the excellencies of Jesus. Note that after urging us "to abstain from the passions of the flesh"—describing the anti-excellent lifestyle—"which wage war against your soul," he goes on to say this: "Keep your conduct among the Gentiles honorable, so that when they speak against you as evildoers, they may see your good deeds and glorify God on the day of visitation" (1 Peter 2:11-12).

In Peter's world, enemies of the Christians spread rumors that they were cannibalistic because they "ate the body and drank the blood of Jesus" at Communion. They faced the slanderous charge that they held orgies in their meetings, because they gathered for "love feasts." They were charged as being insurrectionists and posing a threat to the empire, because they refused to chant "Caesar is Lord" with the crowd. For these charges, they were thrown to the drooling lions and burned on lampposts to light the streets at night. They were called atheists because they did not worship multiple idols, accused of depreciating businesses because they said that slaves were free, and labeled as haters of mankind because they didn't attend the pagan festivals. For all of these charges and others, they became known as "the evildoers." How would they ever prove that they were anything but that?

Or, to fast-forward, how do we stop the hate talk that is aimed at Christians in our own culture? We are marked as the evildoers because we oppose the "progress" that gives women freedom of choice in their reproductive plans, that embraces alternative forms of sexual expression as normative, that seeks to eliminate God from the public square. In fact, we are the only subgroup that is not protected by the PC police. Christians are fair game to be mocked in movies, sitcoms, and music. And we are accused of being arrogant and bigoted when we affirm the words of Jesus that he is the only way to God.

So, how do we make a difference in a world that doesn't particularly like us and our values and certainly doesn't want to hear what we have to say?

Peter gives us a clue: We are to live out the excellencies of Jesus or, as he puts it, "good deeds." We are to do this so that when the world sees us in action, they will glorify God in the day that the consequences of their evil ways come to full fruition. To put it another way, our good works will inspire the culture around us to ultimately glorify God when their way of living comes to empty and negative outcomes and our deeds prove in the end that the "Jesus way" is the right way.

What are these good deeds, and why is it that they have this kind of overcoming power? The Greek word for "good" (*kalos*) in verse 12 is instructive. It means good in terms of visible, winsome expressions of the loving qualities of God through our lives. Or, as one commentator puts it, "goodness that can be seen by others."[2] It bears mentioning that there are other words in the Greek for good deeds. One is *agathos*, which relates to the quality of life as expressed in personal righteousness.

If my observation is correct, most of us have thought that the key to our victory is our unflinching commitment to personal righteousness—*agathos*. Don't misunderstand: I am a raving fan of personal righteousness. But if you are thinking that keeping the rules catches the attention of a hostile world in such a way that they are drawn to see the bankruptcy of their ways and turn to glorify God, you need to reconsider. If I say to someone, "You should become a follower of Jesus so that you, too, could tithe" . . . well, that's going nowhere real fast. Or, "If you become a follower of Jesus, you wouldn't have to sleep around!" Or, "Hey, how would you like to mess up your weekend with church attendance like we do?" So, while personal righteousness is important, it's not the power strategy of the Nation of Jesus. The power is in living lives that are so completely different that even the most resistant pagans say, "I don't get these followers of Jesus, but our town is a better place because they live here." Or a boss who says, "I'm not one of them, but our company is a better company because Jesus followers are employed here."

No wonder Peter uses *kalos* to emphasize external acts of goodness that reflect the deep, rich, and winsome qualities of God. It is this life of reflecting the excellencies of Jesus that makes a difference.

Did you ever wonder how early Christians spread the message of Jesus and grew exponentially in a world where they were marginalized, oppressed, and, worse yet, brutally killed for their allegiance to the true King? Historians tell us that it was their good works that caught the attention of a mocking yet watching world.

As I explained in my book *The Trouble with Jesus*, early Christians fasted to collect their grocery money that they saved to give to the poor. The pagans despised the poor, since the poor couldn't do anything for them in return. Christians showed the excellencies of the King, who himself constantly cared for the poor, the losers, and the lame. The Roman Empire permitted parents to put their unwanted babies on the garbage heaps outside the city gates where they would die from exposure to the elements. Early Christians rescued these babies and raised them for their own. This clearly caught the attention of villagers who saw firsthand that Jesus Nationals were different in meaningful ways.

During the plagues that ravaged the empire, townsfolk fled to the mountains and left their dying relatives to the fate of the plague. Christians stayed in the villages and towns and nursed the dying back to health, at great risk to themselves.

Legend has it that a Roman magistrate called for Saint Lawrence, second-century treasurer of local churches, to bring all the treasures of the church to him. Telling the magistrate that it would take a few days, Lawrence soon showed up with orphans, widows, the blind, the lame, and the poor and said, "Sir, these are the treasures of the church"—for which he was burned on a spit over a bed of coals. As my son-in-law, Pastor Rod Van Solkema, recently said in a sermon, "Early Christians exploited the decadence of their world with acts of goodness that reflected the difference that Jesus makes in a life."

Early Christians were different from those around them. Willing to sacrifice themselves for those who were discarded and uncared for amid a self-centered and sensually accelerated world, the difference in their lives was obvious, compelling, and attractive. They were like Jesus.

We live in a world that, for the most part, does not want to hear what we have to say. But though people might stop listening, you can count on it that they are still watching. This is why Peter says that something happens when people *see* our good works. It is the visibility of our good works that makes others curious about what makes us tick. And when they ask us why we are the way we are, it's an open invitation to tell them about Jesus and to invite them to belong to his nation as well. Increasingly we will have to show up for Jesus before we can speak up for Jesus.

I'm encouraged that there is a growing interest in living out the love of Jesus through intentional acts of *kalos*. Ministries to the homeless, AIDS victims, children at risk; interventions in the rampant sex-slave trade that victimizes stolen children; prison ministries that transform lives; ministries reaching out to immigrants and minority populations; and service to inner-city needs all reflect the rise in programmatic good works in our churches and parachurch ministries. But it's not just the programmatic side of *kalos* that should be in our bag of tricks. I've been thrilled to notice that in times of tragedy and brutal killings, followers of Jesus have reflected in media interviews that they have forgiven the perpetrator of their pain and suffering. To be sure, this kind of response catches the attention of a watching, I-can't-wait-to-get-my-hands-on-those-guys type of world.

A NATION ON A HILL

Peter didn't just come up with this idea on his own. He heard it in a message that Jesus gave in his Sermon on the Mount—the constitution for the Jesus Nation. Peter is simply reiterating the principle that Jesus laid out when he said, "You are the light of the world. A city set on a hill cannot be hidden. Nor do people light a lamp and put it under a basket, but on a stand, and it gives light to all in the house. In the same way, let your light shine before others, so that they may see your good works and give glory to your Father who is in heaven" (Matthew 5:14-16). According to Peter, we have been snatched from darkness and placed into the dazzling presence of Jesus' marvelous light. And, according to Jesus, we are to take this light back into the dark world from which we have come.

But how will a watching world come to glorify God through our good works? What makes our good works any different from the philanthropy of Bill Gates or Warren Buffett, who have both given billions of dollars to good-works projects? The difference is not only in our motivation to proclaim the excellencies of Jesus as representatives of his holy nation but also in our commitment to be sure that a watching world knows that Jesus is the originator of these good works and that as we perform them, we are reflecting his love and concern for the world. The difference is in our giving God the credit when someone pats us on the back or thanks us for a significant act of *kalos*. We *kalos* our world so that people will see our good works *and* glorify our Father in heaven. Which means that even our good works are not about us, but about the Jesus who taught us to live this way.

And, we do good works not just because it's the Jesus way or because we truly care for others. We show God's love to others so that when they run out of steam in their own world, they will seek to know the meaning, purpose, direction, and satisfaction that we have found in Jesus and come to him with a repentant heart to be welcomed into the Jesus Nation. It makes a lot of difference to fill hungry stomachs, and we should. But we will all hunger again. Fill a hungry soul with Jesus, and it will never hunger again! This is the point Jesus was making with the woman at the well. He could have said, "Let me help you draw some of this water; you have a heavy bucket." And I wouldn't be surprised if he had done that, because, unlike some of us, he helped people all the time. But instead Jesus said to her, "Everyone who drinks of this water will be thirsty again, but whoever drinks of the water that I will give him will never be thirsty again. The water that I will give him will become in him a spring of water welling up to eternal life" (John 4:13-14).

GLORY TO GOD

Every day there are opportunities for each us to reach out to others to demonstrate the excellencies of Jesus. There are family members, colleagues at work, and strangers that happen to intersect the trajectory of our lives who are waiting to be touched by a Jesus National. In fact, my recommendation is that you plan to commit one intentional act of *kalos* every day just to stay in shape.

It was six o'clock in the morning, and I had just finished my early run. As I passed the local Starbucks, I decided to stop in and get a couple cups of our favorite lattes and take them home to Martie, who would be waking up. Since the café had just opened, there was only one other person in line in front of me. But it wasn't your ordinary wait-in-line-for-coffee drill. The guy in front of me was in a tense argument with the clerk. In loud and no uncertain terms, the customer was complaining that all he wanted was the copy of the *New York Times* that he was holding in one hand while he was waving a fifty-dollar bill in the other. The fight was over the fact that the clerk did not have enough change yet to break the fifty-dollar bill, which made it impossible for him to sell the paper.

It dawned on me that this was an early morning opportunity to commit one intentional act of *kalos* by demonstrating the excellence of the generous spirit of Jesus. So I said to the clerk, "Hey, put the paper on my bill; I'll buy it for him." This immediately defused the tension, and the grateful *New York Times* guy walked away saying, "Thanks a lot. All I have is yours!" Which evidently did not include the fifty-dollar bill.

To my surprise, when the barista handed me my coffee, he said, "Mister, that was a really nice thing for you to do. This world would be a lot better place to live if more people were like you." What he didn't know was that if he really knew me, he probably wouldn't say that.

His comments caught me totally off guard, and I knew that I could say something at that point that would point the glory upward . . . but nothing came. So I made some self-deprecating remark and walked out, haunted that I had missed a great opportunity to glorify God. As I was walking down the sidewalk, it came to me. I should have said, "Well, this world would not be a better place if more people were like me. But it would be a better place if more people were like Jesus, because he taught me how to do that."

I turned around to go back and tell him that, only to remember that by the time I left there was a line waiting for coffee. It didn't seem to me that it would be a great idea to break into the line and make a religious speech. My only consolation was the thought that I was wearing my Moody Bible Institute hat. So I prayed that he would have noticed my hat. That he would always remember that Bible people do things like that, and that the world would be a better place if there were more Bible people around.

Columnist—and self-proclaimed atheist—Matthew Parris underscores the transforming power that living out the excellence of Jesus can bring to a thirsty culture. In an article in the *London Times*, he draws some stunning conclusions. As a child, he lived in Africa and was personally acquainted with the local missionaries:

The Christians were always different. Far from having cowed or confined its converts, their faith appeared to have liberated and relaxed them. There was a liveliness, a curiosity, an engagement with the world—a directness in their dealings with others—that seemed to be missing in traditional African life. They stood tall.

In his twenties, Parris traveled across the continent with a few other students:

> Whenever we entered a territory worked by missionaries, we had to acknowledge that something changed in the faces of the people we passed and spoke to: something in their eyes, the way they approached you direct, man-to-man, without looking down or away. They had not become more deferential towards strangers—in some ways less so—but more open.

More than forty years later, Parris revisited Malawi—known to him as Nyasaland—and now draws this conclusion:

> . . . Travelling in Malawi refreshed another belief, too: one I've been trying to banish all my life, but an observation I've been unable to avoid since my African childhood. It confounds my ideological beliefs, stubbornly refuses to fit my worldview, and has embarrassed my growing belief that there is no God.
>
> Now a confirmed atheist, I've become convinced of the enormous contribution that Christian evangelism makes in Africa: sharply distinct from the work of secular NGOs, government projects, and international aid efforts. These alone will not do. Education and training alone will not do. In Africa Christianity changes people's hearts. It brings a spiritual transformation. The rebirth is real. The change is good.[3]

Living out the excellencies of Jesus validates the claims of a nation on the move. If you are wondering what will give your life meaning, real change, and lasting significance, wonder no more. Grab that EIL T-shirt and start showing off his excellencies to your world.

Peter has taught us that belonging to the Jesus Nation means that we live to honor him as the preeminent one in our lives. And we do that by living holy, distinctly countercultural lives, so that we can catch the attention of a watching world and draw them into the life-transforming power of our superhero, Jesus. I'd say that's something worth living for. And when I get that right, I'm never bewildered by life. I know exactly what I am supposed to do here. And I never have that hollow ringing sound in my soul that keeps protesting, "There has to be more to life than this!"

Once we rid ourselves of our bewilderment with life and have grasped what it means to belong to the Jesus Nation, we are poised for the adventure of seeing the compelling Jesus for who he really is as we begin the journey of becoming a fully devoted follower of his.

Jesus Nationals understand that life with the King means there are some radical shifts in the way we live. He's number one . . . always. We are different, in a holy sort of way. And we live to show off his excellencies to a watching world. It is these three dynamics that set the stage for living and looking like Jesus—or, as my friend Ed Dobson says, "living Jesusly." So what would behaving Jesusly look like, and how do we get there?

Part 3

BEHAVING JESUSLY

◆

IDENTITY, DIRECTION, AND CONFIDENCE

Chapter 13

KNOWING WHO WE REALLY ARE

ENGLISH LANGUAGE INSTITUTE CHINA (ELIC) is an organization that sends English teachers at the government's request into universities all over Asia in countries like China, Cambodia, Laos, Mongolia, and Vietnam. At a recent conference in Thailand, where all ELIC teachers gathered for their annual conference, I was struck by the statement of one of the teachers. In the closing video, she reflected on a radical change in her life: "From zero to twenty years I was trying to define myself. From twenty-one to eternity I'm living to let Jesus define me." She gets it. As a full-fledged citizen of the Jesus Nation, she knows who she is and who is defining her life.

If we don't know who we really are, then we live with a haunting unsettledness of questions like, Who am I when college is over and all my friends are flying off in different directions and I'm alone in a new career and don't know anyone in the office? Who am I when tragedy strikes and strips away all my props and leaves me in an embarrassing gown in the hospital in pain and fear? Who am I when the children are grown and gone and I am home alone? Who am I when I have been a high-level businessperson and then I am let go . . . or I retire . . . or I'm not the president of the company anymore? Who am I when death takes my spouse of many years and the most important person in my life is gone? Who am I when I'm married to a high-profile person and all the attention goes to him or her, and I am left in the shadows?

Without a clear sense of identity, we are left to wander through life needing to redefine ourselves and feeling that deep in our core we are never quite sure who we really are. And when we are not sure who we really are, then we let friends, position, titles on our business cards, seasons of life, hormones and instincts, husbands or wives, whims and trends, and a whole bunch of other influences define us, which only leaves us confused about ourselves and headed for less-than-desirable outcomes.

If you and I could meet and spend a few minutes getting acquainted, in the course of our conversation I'd probably ask you who you are. Most likely I'd get the butcher, baker, candlestick-maker kind of response. But I would have to tell you that what you do is not who you are. Because if what you do is who you are, who will you be when you don't do that anymore? And if we could go deep, I'd want to tell you that in the Jesus Nation we know exactly who we are because Jesus gives us a lifelong identity that both drives and defines our lives regardless of our season in life, unexpected events, change, or tragedy.

Knowing who you actually are isn't a throwaway issue. It's a serious matter, because our sense of identity shapes and defines our lives. You might be an executive in a downtown office, and that sense of identity dictates the clothes you buy, the pens you use, what you talk about, the places you go for lunch, and a host of other life-defining realities. But that's not who you are. If all you think of yourself is that you are a homemaker, an executive, a farmer, a professional athlete, or whatever it is, then you have missed something very important. Homemaking is what you do and where you do it. It has nothing to do with who you really are. In fact, you will be a really crummy homemaker if you are a really crummy person. Same thing goes for being a doctor, a Baptist, a homeless person, or a financial wizard.

Margaret Thatcher, former prime minister of England, is said to have visited a nursing home in one of her campaigns. After shaking hands with many of the residents, she noticed a lady sitting in the corner in a wheelchair, totally disengaged. She went over and extended her hand only to be greeted with a rather disinterested gaze. She finally said to the lady, "Do you know who I am?" To which the woman responded, "No, but the nurse over there helps us with that kind of thing."

Jesus wants to help us with who we are.

NEW IDENTITY

In an early encounter with four rugged fishermen, Jesus welcomed them to a whole new identity, one that would be steady and definitive for them for the rest of their lives, an identity that would give them a life of adventure and significance, that would lead them to affect the world for generations to come. If you had met Andrew, Peter, James, or John on the street in their little fishing village in Galilee and had asked them who they were, they would no doubt have said, "Thanks for asking. We are fishermen."

Jesus was about to change all of that.

Matthew records the life-changing moment. Speaking of Jesus, he writes, "While walking by the Sea of Galilee, he saw two brothers, Simon (who is called Peter) and Andrew his brother, casting a net into the sea, for they were fishermen. And he said to them, 'Follow me, and I will make you fishers of men.' Immediately they left their nets and followed him" (Matthew 4:18-20).

Jesus goes on to offer the same honor to James and John, who were mending nets in the boat with their father Zebedee. The offer was simple yet life-changingly profound. They could hang with fish and do the same thing over and over, day after day, or they could get past the nets and hear some amazing truths that would captivate their minds and confound the Bible bureaucrats and watch the lame walk again, the religious hypocrites burn with envy, and the dead come to life. Their choice.

And his offer to you is the same. It's your choice. You can stay stuck in the old routines and keep hoping that someday you will win the lottery, or you can unstick yourself and let Jesus make something of your life. You can follow Jesus and, surprisingly, find that there is something more exhilarating than living life your way, in the confines of your instincts.

I find it interesting that "follow me" is the first thing that Jesus said to Peter and also one of the last things Jesus said to him (see John 21:19). Being a follower of Jesus is the identity that bookends our journey through life. It is the essence of authentic Christianity and the common identity that is shared by Jesus Nationals.

So it is no surprise that the central theme of Jesus' encounter with these fishermen is *following*. Jesus is about ready to stamp them with a new identity. They will no longer be fishermen; that occupation of theirs will come and go. They are now *followers of Jesus*—an identity that will drive and define them for the rest of their lives.

If you had said to me as we were getting acquainted, "Thanks for asking. I'm a follower of Jesus," you would have hit the nail on the head. But before we unwrap what it means for us to live out our identity as followers of Jesus, there are a couple of resistance points that we need to come to grips with.

I can almost feel you breaking into a cold sweat thinking, "He's going to ask me to give up my career and be a missionary to some snake-infested, backwater pagan tribe." Relax! Following Jesus doesn't mean that you will give up your job security. Jesus needs you, as his follower, to live out your identity right where you work and in the town where you live. To be honest, following him might mean a change of location and profession. But not always. And believe me, if he has a change in mind for you, you are in the wrong place, anyway. He wants to locate you right where you are supposed to be.

But the bigger resistance point has to do with the concept of following, to begin with. Envisioning yourself as a follower is counterintuitive. No one wants to be a follower, not really. Most of us would far rather think of ourselves in terms of fame, fortune, or nice places to live. Followers, in our eyes, are somewhere toward the bottom of the food chain of existence. Our world is inebriated with the pursuit of leadership as the highest level of achievement. Go into any bookstore, and it will be really tough to find a book on followership. All the best sellers are about how to lead and to manage your life to stay on top of the pile. Leaders tell people what to do and get the applause for everyone else's work. Who wouldn't want a job like that? Followers are the drones. The unnoticed minions.

But even if you are a leader, to do it well you need to be a follower. We have all seen spiritual leaders fall. It's a tragic event with massive repercussions for the family, the ministry, and the reputation of Jesus in our world. But I have to tell you that I have never seen a leader fail because he or she didn't know how to lead. Leaders fail because at some point in their lives they failed to be a devoted follower of Jesus.

After eighteen years of serving at the Moody Bible Institute in Chicago, I came to the realization that my work there was done. Soon after I announced my decision, a well-meaning friend came to me and said, "How can you do this? You're the president of Moody. You just can't walk away from that. Who will you be?" The answer to that question is that I will be who I was before I came to Moody, who I strove to be while leading Moody. It's who I am at Cornerstone University and who I will be long after Cornerstone—a follower of Jesus.

When you are tempted to reject the idea of being a follower, remember that in reality we are all followers of something or someone. Sometimes it's an influential professor, a trendy book, a friend, or a lover. But when push comes to shove, we are most likely to crown ourselves as the leader of our lives. And when that happens we become unquestioning followers of our egos and our instincts. We become slaves to our inner voices. But claiming to be a "follower of me" is a real spooky thought. As we have noted, we are born fallen, and as such, our ego is always out of whack, and our first instincts are often wrong.

If you offend me, my first instinct is not to forgive you and get on with my life. My first instinct is to figure out a way to get back, which only escalates into a bigger war, given the fact that you are not inclined to forgive and get on with your life, either. And now both of us are stuck in the past and preoccupied with a battle that no one will win. Even if you could follow your ego and instincts and avoid all the train wrecks, in the end your life would have that hollow ring to it that always is the endgame of folks who have dedicated themselves to themselves for the rest of their lives.

The choice is not whether I will be a follower, but rather, who I can trust enough to follow.

In my freshman year in college, there was a sophomore by the name of B.J. on our floor. Late in the evening, he would gather us in his room and help us concoct mischievous schemes to execute under the cover of night. With our adrenaline running high, we would run out of his room and pull off our late-night campus pranks only to get caught repeatedly getting ourselves in deep trouble. What we finally realized was that B.J. never went out with us. He set us up and took great delight in seeing freshmen in the tank.

I learned that B.J. was a leader that I couldn't trust to follow. And that wasn't the only time I learned the hard way that I had chosen the wrong leadership in my life. But after many years of my following Jesus, he has never let me down.

So what does it mean for a Jesus National to follow Jesus? One thing I'm struck by is how life changing this call is. First, the call is a formula.

Jesus says, "Follow me, and I will make you fishers of men." Unfortunately, most of us are pretty lame when it comes to getting Bible formulas straight. For instance, Paul writes that "to live is Christ, and to die is gain" (Philippians 1:21). It's a formula. But to watch our lives, it is clear that we have it backward. We live for gain and believe that Jesus will be really important when we die. No wonder our lives are so full of emptiness. Or, take Paul's words: "godliness with contentment is great gain" (1 Timothy 6:6, NIV). We twist that formula, living as though godliness plus gain would make us content, only to struggle with the unsolvable tension between the true pursuit of godliness and the pursuit of a life that is all about bigger piles and better stuff. Getting God's formulas out of sync always gets our Christianity out of sync as well.

So, let's get this one straight. In essence, Jesus says, "Follow me and let me make something of your life." It's a transfer of your interest from fishing—or whatever it is that distracts you from the call—to the needs of people and netting them for Jesus. But, if you are like a lot of us, we start by saying, "I'm going to make something of my life!" And then we go to church and hear that we are to follow Jesus, so we say, "OK, while I'm making something of my life, I'll try to follow him." Backwards!

He calls you so that he can make your life something that really counts, now and for eternity. It's not that he doesn't want you to have dreams and passions. He just knows that if those dreams eclipse your commitment to following him, then you will follow your dreams and not him. And following him is always best.

As I am writing this, Martie and I are just completing a transition in our lives. I recently finished serving as a teaching pastor in a Chicago church to take the position of president of Cornerstone University in Grand Rapids, Michigan. High on our list of things to do after moving was finding a good doctor. Our doctor in Chicago had given us outstanding care, and in our minds, the chances of finding a great replacement were slim. But a friend made a recommendation and called ahead to help us make an appointment. We arrived and were treated to a tour of the medical practice by one of the nurses. Along the way, she told us that "Dr. Sam always wants to be sure that his patients understand that he simply facilitates the work of 'the Great Physician.'" Telling the story of a patient who had complimented the doctor on a major turnaround in her health following surgery, the nurse quoted the doctor as assuring the patient that it wasn't he who had accomplished the healing; he had just moved a few things around and had sewn them up. He told her that he had just cooperated with the amazing work of the Creator, who had built a body with all the systems necessary to make healing a possibility in the first place.

After the tour and the unashamed giving of credit and glory to God, we met with "Dr. Sam." As he described his practice and his approach to medicine, he mentioned his involvement with a ministry to the inner city that provides medical services to those without medical insurance.

I left the office that day thinking that I had met a member of the Jesus Nation who understood the identity of an authentic Christian. We are first and foremost followers of Jesus—followers who let Jesus make something significant of our lives, who live for far better things that transcend our own self-interests and use our careers to magnify Jesus. And if you asked Dr. Sam, I am sure that he would say that living out his true identity in Jesus beats a life that is dead-ended into a wall of framed credentials, playing cards at the country club, and getting all the applause for something that he could never have done on his own.

Businesspeople who are first and foremost followers of Jesus let him make something of their lives by being people of integrity and loyalty, contributing an honest day's work that resonates to his glory and fame. Jesus Nationals boycott gossip sessions at the watercooler. They show up on time. They advance the values and uphold the standards of the company.

Parents who are followers of Jesus see their roles as a platform from which to show and teach their children about Jesus—and not just about his saving grace but also about his character and the advancement of his mission in our world. Followers see the homeless, the poor, and the oppressed as opportunities to demonstrate the compassion of Jesus, not as objects of criticism and scorn . . . or worse yet as those not worthy of our attention.

I have a friend who has the Midas touch. It's remarkable. He works hard *and* is massively rewarded. I have watched his high level of energy and type A passion with admiration. So, he had my full attention when he once said to me, "Joe, do you know why I work like this?" When I couldn't come up with a response, he quickly said, "To support my habit!" I felt like he was getting ready to confess something dark, but he continued, "My habit is to advance the cause of Christ in this world. The more I make, the more I can give away!" He's a follower, and Jesus is making something significant of his life. Just ask the thousands who have been touched by his generosity.

But it's not just rich folks who find that Jesus can make something significant of their lives. Whoever you are, and wherever you go, there are opportunities to follow Jesus beyond your own little world. Opportunities to forgive an enemy, care for a neighbor, be generous in spirit, have compassion for the lost, invest in eternity, volunteer at an out-of-the-way ministry with out-of-the-way people, reach out to that person in the cubicle next to you at work who has a serious need, or let people cut in front of you in traffic without wanting to flip them off or even blasting them with your horn. As a Jesus National, you simply take your cues from the leader, and something significant begins to take shape in your life.

Actualizing your true identity as a Jesus National simply means that you let Jesus determine the trajectory of your life, a trajectory that will ultimately delight you with a life that has meaning and significance. Getting lost in the wonder, ways, and will of Jesus finally takes us out of the stagnant air of "me" and launches us into the fresh air of life in him.

So if you are looking for an upgrade in life, let me welcome you to the privilege of being a follower. It's your choice: Do you want to be an angry, vengeful person or a grace-full and forgiving one? Antsy and quick-tempered or patient? Proud, boastful, and obnoxious—or dynamically humble and attractive? Self-centered or interested in others? Consumed by stuff and the accumulation of piles of soon-to-be-junk—or consumed by people and the joy of building strong, satisfying relationships? Smart, well-educated, and successful because you are so clever—or would you like to top all that by having wisdom? Would you want to leave a big inheritance or a compelling legacy? Have credentials or character? Greed or generosity? Be unmoved by the plight of the oppressed, the poor, and the marginalized—or be merciful and just? Tell me to stop . . . I have a word limit here . . . the list could go on. Enough said, though. You only get true purely motivated grace, forgiveness, patience, humility, concern for others, wisdom, legacy, generosity, mercy, justice, and a non-materialistic view of life from Jesus. You might be able to fire up for a few of these on your own now and then, but the whole package, the unmitigated-by-circumstances real deal, is only from Jesus.

It's all about the formula. Follow Jesus, and let him make something of your life.

It had to be really tough for Peter and Andrew to leave all that was familiar and predictable. They knew how to fish, and they were good at it. Tougher yet for James and John to leave the family business. So it really stuns me that in each case, they *immediately* left it all to follow him.

You have to live in this passage. Put on your sandals and fish-stained robe and engage with them as Jesus throws out this new option for their lives. The fact that they immediately leave it all to follow him is amazing. You and I would want to discuss this a little further. Is it long term or short term? Can I visit my mother on weekends? Is there a 401(k) plan? I know that we would have a lot of questions and would like some time to process it all. So the fact that they left it all immediately catches my attention.

It tells me that Jesus is a very compelling person! We have already seen that he is like a magnet to these tough fishermen, tax collectors, members of the resistance force, doctors, scholars, and to regular folk like us. So whatever you think of Jesus, make sure that the word *compelling* is on the list. They gave it all up for him, and though there were tough and confusing times, they never looked back and in the end were not disappointed.

But there is something more than meets the eye here.

THE PRIVILEGE OF FOLLOWING

IF YOU THINK that life as a follower is some kind of second-rate assignment that sticks you at the bottom of the ladder with footprints of leaders embedded in your face, think again. There's a reason these tough fishermen didn't think twice when Jesus made the offer.

Don't yawn here! Miss this point, and you'll miss what's so compelling about being a follower.

These guys were no doubt in their late teens and would have already been fully engaged in their fishing business for several years . . . at least since they were about twelve or thirteen. That's when they would have graduated out of Sabbath school. Ever since they were able to read, Jewish boys would sit at the feet of the local rabbi every Saturday to learn the ways of God and what it meant to be Jewish. Lessons from the Torah were exhaustive, and well-spun stories about the greats of Jewish history—the likes of Abraham, Moses, and David—were the features *du jour.* Every Jewish boy was jammed full of Jewishness.

Once they were finished with Sabbath school, the outstanding students, the really brilliant ones, would get the honor of asking the rabbi if they could become one of his followers. There was no higher honor in Judaism than to have the rabbi choose you to follow him. Followers were welcome to move into the rabbinic compound and to sit at the rabbi's feet while he taught. They would count it the highest honor to serve him in even the most menial tasks.

A friend tells me that in Orthodox Judaism today, followers still exist as the privileged few, and the attitude of privilege extends far: even to counting it the highest honor to wash the rabbi's undergarments. No task too small or too large for the service of the rabbi! They listened to his every word, watched his every move, analyzed his thought process, and knew in their hearts that the only way to get to God was to get as close as possible to their local rabbi.

Everyone wanted the privilege, but only a select few got to get up close and personal. It was a passionate attachment; the rabbi was a follower's sole focus in life. Followers would be so taken with their rabbi that they would begin to dress, look, and act like the rabbi. In fact, if there were more than one rabbi in town, you could tell which rabbi a follower was connected to by simply watching him act and listening to how he talked. Ed, a friend of mine who travels to Israel regularly, tells of the time he was near the Wailing Wall and noticed an old rabbi walking by. Crooked and bent over with age, he walked leaning on his cane, tilting to the right as though one leg were shorter than the other. Ed noticed that walking behind the aged rabbi was a group of his young followers, bent over with canes and walking with a self-induced tilt to the right.

When Jesus calls us to follow him, these dynamics are what he has in mind. We don't begin to satisfy our souls with the presence of God until we get up close and personal with him. As he clearly says, "No one comes to the Father except through me" (John 14:6). As followers of his, we are to listen to all that he says and teaches, to observe his every move, to track his thought process, and to so admire him that we start looking like him.

I have a colleague who is so committed to being a devoted follower that this year he is reading through the Gospels once each week to catch a clear vision of the will and ways of Jesus. He wants to passionately pursue Jesus with intentional awareness of who Jesus really is. What a great idea!

Early followers did this so well that their culture gave them a nickname: *Christians.* They didn't get it from gathering in a room with a whiteboard to figure out a cool new logo. It was from having acted and spoken so much like Jesus that the world called them "Christ ones." What is there about your life that would clearly mark you as a privileged follower of Jesus? If you find yourself scratching your head, don't stop reading! We are going to look closely at the adventure of following him in the pages to come. Believe me, on this adventure you won't be bored. Challenged? Yes. Bored? No!

Meanwhile, back at the fishing village . . .

The less-than-brilliant ones in Sabbath school did not get the privilege of asking to follow their rabbi. They went to work with their fathers in the trades. In this case, they became fishermen. So put yourself in their place. Like kids in high school who have tried out for the championship football team or the cheerleading squad, on the day the roster is posted on the locker-room door, they walk by and don't see their names. They didn't make the cut! Their dreams are dashed. So for these four graduates of Sabbath school, going fishing was not a thrilling option. It was simply all that was left. The default position in life.

So, in the midst of the routine of their lives, Jesus shows up on the beach and asks them to become his followers. We can only imagine what that would have meant to this boatload of second-rate former Sabbath school students. For one thing, in Jesus' time, rabbis never asked anyone to follow them. That would not be rabbinical. One had to come hat in hand, asking the rabbi for the privilege, knowing all the time that he would probably be refused. Like a guy asking that cool girl out on a date, all the time harboring the fear that she would turn him down. But what if that gorgeous girl, who he never dreamed could be interested in someone the likes of himself, would walk up to him with a sparkle in her eyes and say she wanted to get to know him? That's the beginning of life in a far better place! These guys relegated to the trades would have felt something like that when Jesus called them to follow him.

Think of what an important moment this was for these fishermen. While they are at work, absorbed in the routine of their nets and bobbers, there is a sound behind them. Someone is breaking into their zone. They look up, and it's Jesus . . . the headline-making rabbi who is just starting to catch the attention of the muckety-mucks in Jerusalem. This Jesus, unlike other rabbis who wouldn't have lowered themselves to ask anyone to follow them, is now making an astounding offer. He is asking them . . . the losers . . . to follow him! It's deeply significant, when you understand all the ramifications. They wouldn't even think of saying, "Well, thanks for the offer. We like you a lot, but we are really into fish right now." No way!

That's why they left it all. For the sheer honor of the upgrade that he offered them. In time, they would be taken with him for himself and learn to lose themselves in his preeminence. But for now they were simply losers no more. They left it all and followed him, and our world has never been the same. They fanned the fires of a newfound faith that burns to this day. In fact, you and I owe—in a human sense—our eternal destinies to these early followers. Talk about letting Jesus make something of your life!

It's important to connect the dots. We have a lot in common with these fishermen. Before God, we all make a failing grade. When it comes to being able to launch a soul-satisfying relationship with God, we don't make the cut. Worse yet, we *can't* make the cut. Unlike Jewish school, there is not one of us worthy of the honor on our own. We are the true losers, with no hope of ever sharing the honor of life in close proximity to the rabbi of our souls. But this compelling Jesus shows up on the beach of our hearts, welcomes us into his nation, calls us to the high honor of being numbered among his followers, and crowns us with significance. A significance not in our own attainments, but in the fact that we, the undeserving ones, have been called by Jesus to the privilege of becoming followers of him.

What's holding you back from leaving it all behind? Are you really that much into fish? Or, I should ask, what's with those nets in your hand?

I've read the account of Jesus' call for Peter and Andrew to follow him many times. But I'll never forget the time I read it and noticed the "net talk" in the interchange. Matthew could have recorded that they immediately followed him. But he adds that immediately they *left their nets* and followed him. It dawned on me in a moment of conviction that as long as they were hanging onto their nets, they were going nowhere with Jesus. The conviction came when I realized that I had nets that I needed to drop, as well.

What are our "nets"? Anything that inhibits or prohibits our capacity to be fully devoted followers of Jesus. So before we go much further in our journey as followers of Jesus, we need to examine the nets that are tangled in our hands. They could be just about anything: secret sins, desires that conflict with his, refusal to forgive a deep offense, self-centered pursuits that collide with his call for us to serve others . . . I don't know what your nets are. I just know we all have them and that Jesus calls us to leave them behind so that we are free to follow. Followers are netless believers!

Obviously, dropping our nets is not a once-in-a-lifetime action. You will find that once you are on the road with Jesus, your adversary will offer you a little net from behind a bush at the side of the trail. He will tell you that no one is netless all the time, that you deserve a net once in a while. In fact, he will whisper, "It's just a small net; you can walk and carry it at the same time." So you reach out and take it . . . only to find that you really can't follow Jesus and be tangled up in your net at the same time, regardless of its size. To truly follow him, we have to keep dropping our nets all the way home.

I'd like to think that when you get up from reading this book, wherever you are, people will notice the pile of nets on the floor where you were sitting. If they ask you what they are, just tell them that they are the things that once held you back from embarking on the greatest adventure in life.

Netless nationals are proud to be followers. We live for it. But figuring out how to live that way in our everyday experience is the next challenge.

WAY-MAKER JESUS

THE WORD FOR "FOLLOWING" in the Gospels literally means "to be *found in the way*" with him. I love the word pictures that come to mind: Way-maker Jesus, Path-treader Jesus. Jesus came into our world and refused to walk in the highly gridlocked, deeply rutted ways of this world. Instead, with the machete of his wisdom, he cut new paths through the jungle of life. New ways that he walked with creativity, courage, and consistency. And just in case we missed the point, he made a spectacular claim when he was here with us. He said without embarrassment, "I am the way" (John 14:6).

As we have already noted, for most of our lives you and I have thought that he meant that he was the way to heaven—which, of course, is wonderfully true. But it's also more than that. When he said, "I am the way," he literally meant that he is *the* way. He is the way to do all of life and everything in life. So for three intensive years, Jesus lived to show us the way in which we should do life in his nation. And though his way is new and often counterintuitive, he cut the way and walked in it. And he looks over his shoulder to see if any of us are in the way with him or if we are wandering off to some side road that leads to nowhere. He knows where he is going, and he wants you to be in the way with him.

Writing this reminds me of the times my dad used to take me to the circus. As we would walk down the midway toward the big tent, the path would be lined with sideshows. For a quarter you could go behind the advertising tarp and see a bearded lady, a sword swallower, a guy with three eyes, a two-headed snake—lots of opportunities to have your curiosity distract you from the reason you were there in the first place: the main event. I used to beg my dad to let me go into the sideshows, and he would always say, "Joe, that's a waste of money"—which is exactly what I didn't want to hear! So, the first time I went to the circus on my own I headed straight for the sideshow tents, only to lay out the cash and realize that it wasn't all it was cracked up to be. As my almost-always-right dad had said, it was a waste of money.

There are a lot of sideshows seducing us to get off the way with Jesus. Some aren't necessarily bad; some are devastatingly bad; but all are serious distractions. Whether it's living only to advance our careers, charging ourselves into financial oblivion for the lure of all that glitters, side trips to Pornville, or loving to hate, there are countless opportunities to duck behind the flap of an alluring sideshow. But it's always more costly than we think. As for me, I'll stay on the road with Jesus. He's headed for the big show! Remember, he knows where he is going, and he wants to take us there.

So, what would it look like if you and I were on the way with him?

Frankly, it's hard to know where to start, since his ways are so distinctively different and all-encompassing. Whether to start with thoughts or attitudes or reactions or relationships or money or emotions or any other of his compelling ways is a challenge. But if you demanded that I tell you about his ways in three words or less, I would tell you that the clearest thing I know about it is that *people matter most*! And if you would get beyond the three-word limit, I would say that he was passionate about one commodity on this planet, and that was people. All kinds of people.

FOLLOWERS SHARE HIS PASSION FOR PEOPLE

For all of us who think that following Jesus means we should tithe more, send our kids to the mission field, stop watching bad stuff on TV or the computer, work in the church nursery, or pray more, we're wrong. That's the easy stuff.

As important as all of that might be, it's people—their needs and nurture—that really matter most with Jesus. I realize that this sounds discouraging to many of us. I have always thought that life would be a cakewalk if it weren't for people. But that's just it: People are a needy commodity, and Jesus came to help them. All the way from rescuing them from the bondage of hell to giving them food, clothing, healing, encouragement, instruction, and anything else that can get people up and running in the right direction.

Remember the first big crash that left us wandering aimlessly on this "island"? We've all been in a bad wreck with sin, but Jesus came to restore us to the original glory that he intended for us before sin smacked the daylights out of us. From our spouses to our children; to our colleagues at work; to friends, enemies, liberals, conservatives, prostitutes, criminals, bosses, and employees. All people are objects of Jesus' abiding interest and concern.

This passion for helping and serving people is clear from the very beginning. The prophets forecast that the Messiah would come to save people from their sins. When Jesus called the first disciples, he made it clear that he was upgrading them from filleting fish to helping people. And just in case they missed the point, as soon as they left their nets, he led them to people in Galilee, where he taught and healed the likes of the lame, epileptic, and a host of other hurting people (see Matthew 4:23-25).

Jesus apparently had no interest in taking his new recruits up to Jerusalem so that the people with power could leverage his ministry. He was not into massaging egos and giving them a few names to drop now and then. It's not that the higher-ups don't count with Jesus; it's just that he wasn't about to get trapped in their web of politicking and networking. The world of leveraging power for personal advancement was innately foreign to him. If you will let me digress here, I can't resist the temptation to remind you of his trial in the wilderness.

Power to the people.

Having fasted for forty days and nights, tired, hungry, and depleted, Jesus was offered some pretty nifty opportunities by none other than the arch-deceiver himself, Satan. The last time Satan had actually shown up in person was in the spectacular confines of Eden. Into the beauty and the unrestrained satisfaction of uncomplicated and fulfilling relationships, Satan offered his wares in such a compelling way that the first pair took the bait. You know the rest of the story. Satan didn't hang around to make them happy as he had promised he would; he slithered off, leaving them lost in regret and shame.

Has a familiar ring, doesn't it? Not only the entire human race, but all of creation fell under a destructive curse (see Romans 8:19-23). I find it interesting and instructive that, when Satan first entered God's territory, he entered a garden of unrestrained beauty and joy. And when Jesus enters Satan's territory, it's a barren, wild wasteland. At Satan's first appearance, Adam and Eve are Exhibit A of the good life—at least, they would have been models of health in a glorious Eden. At the tempter's second appearance, Jesus is wasted and tired after a forty-day fast, preparing himself for the pressing challenge of ministering in a fallen world.

It is to this frail Jesus that Satan offers three temptations: Use your power to "feed yourself"; "Do something spectacular with your power"; "Worship me (transfer your power to me), and I'll give to you now what you otherwise have to suffer to get!" (see Matthew 4:1-10).

Unwrapping these to great extent would be a book in itself, so let me get right to the point. With literally hundreds of rocks surrounding Jesus in the wilderness, Satan encouraged him to use his power to feed himself from them. Innocent enough. But if Jesus would do that, he would be using his power to bless and help himself. In this case, it might not have been a big deal. But it would establish a pattern that would be lethal to his future ministry. Such a pattern might include using his power to mow down the Roman soldiers in the garden (think of the special effects!), or calling ten thousand angels to take him off the cross. Jesus knew that God had given him his power to bless and benefit others, not himself. If he was going to trigger the power of food making, it would be to feed five thousand hungry men plus women and children.

Or what about the offer to jump off the Temple tower and prove his deity by having angels set out a rescue net for him on the sidewalk? I can just hear Satan saying, "Look at you! All shriveled up and gaunt. No one will ever follow you in that condition. Do something spectacular. Get into that phone booth and let's see those blue tights and the red shirt with the *S* for SuperMessiah! Live for the applause of the crowd!" But again, Jesus would have none of it. He didn't come to be SuperMessiah. He came to be the superservant. If he would do something spectacular, he would do it to help someone else . . . someone suffering from blindness, deafness, demon possession, sin, or even death.

Persistent as he is, Satan had one more offer up his sleeve. A deal that

Satan thought Jesus couldn't refuse. After showing him all the kingdoms of the world and their glory from a high mountain, Satan made his best offer yet: "All these I will give you, if you will fall down and worship me" (Matthew 4:9). Satan already knew that Jesus would someday be Lord of every nation and subdue hostile rulers and nations under his feet in final victory (see 1 Corinthians 15:24-28). But he also knew that Jesus would have to suffer defeat and a torturous death to get it done.

What a convenient shortcut! "I can have it all now—just a little dip of the knee to this clever guy and it's mine." Sound familiar? "Just a little compromise here won't hurt anyone, and I can have what I really want." A moment of thrill in an affair, some extra cash by giving in to Satan's temptation to cheat on a contract, safety for lying my way out of trouble. But if Jesus had taken this shortcut, he would never have been able to set us captives free from our sins and to birth the nation he came to build. The shortcuts that Satan offers always end up satisfying us for a short time—and short-circuiting people who desperately need our help. Think of children who have been cheated out of a father because theirs decided to bow to the salesman of destruction and satisfy himself with an affair. Or of customers who have lost money or who are stuck with a poor product because someone discovered a nifty way to line his or her own pockets at their expense.

Jesus knew that he had to suffer to win, surrender to gain, and die so that others could live. Besides, it wasn't the fleeting, glitzy nations of the world and their deep treasuries that he was after. The glitter wouldn't distract him. He came to make a whole new nation, whose glory would be in followers of his who would find satisfaction in him forever!

Jesus didn't come to use his power to satisfy himself, to wow the crowds, or to gather up piles of stuff from the kingdoms of this world. He came to use his power to enable and enhance others, so that God might be glorified and needy, failing hearts would be drawn to his saving grace and the transforming power of his gospel.

Jesus chose people over tradition.

To Jesus, people mattered more—not only more than his own self-interest, but also more than religious rules and traditions. Think of how often he got nailed by the religious leaders of his day for making the blind to see on the wrong day of the week or in the wrong way. And what about the Sabbath police who got their boxers in a bunch when the disciples picked heads of wheat to eat? Or what about when Jesus healed people on the Sabbath and had to resort to saying things that should be as plain as the nose on your face like "The Sabbath was made for man, not man for the Sabbath" (Mark 2:27) or "Which of you, having a son or an ox that has fallen into a well on a Sabbath day, will not immediately pull him out?" (Luke 14:5). Think of how he got hammered because he blatantly forgave sinners without having them jump through all the hoops of the Temple traditions.

He proved it time and again. Above all else, people matter most.

But he was up against a twisted way of looking at people. In Jesus' day, religious people held at arm's length anyone who was not like them. There was a subtle suspicion that people who were different were dangerous. And if people wanted to be included, they needed to become like those in the religious club and then prove themselves before they could be accepted. In effect, the unwritten rule was that you had to *behave* like them, then you had to *believe* like them; and if those two things were in place, you stood a pretty good chance of *belonging* to them.

Jesus systematically dismantled the well-worn "Good Guys versus Bad Guys" paradigm. He made it clear that all people were welcome to enter into his love and companionship. That's what got him into so much trouble with the church leaders. They constantly held against him— and tried to use against him—the fact that he ate with tax collectors and sinners (see Luke 15:1-2). And it was an irritation to them that he was an advocate for repentant prostitutes and Samaritans. But because these needy people felt welcome in his company, their proximity to Jesus turned into belief, and when that belief began to mature, they behaved differently. So Jesus' pattern was that people mattered most, expressed in the fact that everyone felt like they belonged in his presence, which meant that they could believe in his message so that they could behave in ways that reflected their newfound faith in him.

You probably know some churches and Christian groups that still do the behave-believe-belong routine. Some bad habits are hard to kill. But if you are a follower of Jesus, you have a different approach. To everyone. With Jesus it is always belonging . . . so that you can believe . . . so that you can behave.

Nowhere is this people-matter-most, belong-believe-behave dynamic more profoundly expressed than in the encounter we have mentioned briefly before, between Jesus and a Samaritan woman at the well.

In John 4 we read that after a long journey, Jesus rests by Jacob's well as his disciples go into the city of Sychar to get lunch to go. The fact that they are in Sychar is a problem. It means that they are in Samaria, which is enemy territory. It must have been a real beard stroker when Jesus told them that they had to go home through Samaria. If you were Jewish, you normally would have taken a detour to avoid the discomfort of running into Samaritans. Jews and Samaritans had long-term disdain for each other, which ups the ante for what is about to happen.

As Jesus rests by the well around noon, a woman approaches to draw water. Her entrance onto the stage creates massive problems for Jesus. First, no rabbi worth his Torah would stay at the well upon her arrival. Rabbis refused to been seen in public with women. Women were sources of seduction, mere chattel in the social structure. If a woman was approaching a rabbi on a village road, he would move to the other side of the road until she passed and then resume his journey. For Jesus to remain was a significant risk to his reputation.

Besides that fact, she was a Samaritan. This injects an ethnic-political tension into the moment. Then add the significant fact that Jesus knew she had been through five marriages and was now living with a sixth man.

In fact, her coming at noon indicates that she is a marginalized woman. Women normally came to the well in the evening. Water drawing was a social event, and men came to strike up conversations and perhaps kindle a little romance. This woman's arrival at noon indicates that she was shunned by the other women. We are not sure why, but perhaps she has been cast out because of her multiple marriages.

At any rate, Jesus is now faced with a seriously awkward moment. Jewish pride ran deep, and with it came deep prejudices. She isn't "their kind of people." Their traditions had been elevated to the level of binding law: Rabbis don't get caught in situations like this. So, if Jesus stays, he's in a peck of trouble.

He stays.

Not only that, but he initiates the conversation. It's no awkward-look-at-the-ground-and-pretend-you're-sleeping trick for Jesus. Breaking through the barriers of prejudice, tradition, and personal pride, he goes after her need—which, interesting enough, wasn't the water in the well but the "water" that Jesus could give to her thirsty soul. What she couldn't find in the marriage mall, Jesus would provide for her that day at the well. As he said, the water that he would give her was living water. When she is amazed that a Jewish man would strike up a conversation with her—given the romantic implications of men hanging out at the well, I wonder if she thought, *Oh no, here it goes; I'm getting hit on again!*—he says in response, "If you knew the gift of God, and who it is that is saying to you, 'Give me a drink,' you would have asked him, and he would have given you living water. . . . Everyone who drinks of this water will be thirsty again, but whoever drinks of the water that I will give him will never be thirsty again. The water that I will give him will become in him a spring of water welling up to eternal life" (John 4:10, 13-14).

With Jesus, people and their needs matter most regardless of personal pride, prevailing prejudices, and unforgiving traditions. Even if he had to put himself at risk with the prejudice police and the tradition cops.

And in case you think I'm exaggerating, a brief look at the disciples' response confirms the tension. John tells us that when the disciples returned, they "marveled" that he would be talking to a woman (see John 4:27). They were no doubt marveling in an astonished sort of way, as if to say, "Doesn't he know that he's wrecking everything? If people find out about this back in Jerusalem, our whole mission will go down the drain!" Well, actually I can't be sure that it was that kind of marveling, but that probably would have been my response. What is clear, however, is that according to John they didn't ask the obvious question: "Why are you talking to her?" But they did say, "We brought you lunch!" Jesus said he wasn't hungry, that he had food to eat that they didn't know about. He meant that he was so into the excitement of meeting the woman's need and doing the will of his Father that he wasn't hungry anymore. To which they responded, "Did someone bring him lunch?"

Clearly they didn't get it. They were into their picnic; Jesus was into people. They were into their needs; Jesus was into others' needs. They saw the Samaritan woman through the lens of their prejudices and traditions; Jesus saw her far differently. Her need was more important to him than anything else in his life. More important than his reputation, and more important than his lunch!

A few years ago, a fad swept America that drove me nuts. Magic Eye pictures ended up everywhere. They were full of squiggly lines and tiny shapes. At first glance, they made no sense at all. At best, they looked like random designs. But if you stood in front of one and concentrated, so I'm told, you could begin to see a picture emerge. I would stand there for a long time, looking for the palm-lined beach and the dolphins jumping from the sea. To no avail . . . ever. But Martie could step up to a Magic Eye picture and almost immediately see the picture emerge. She could always see it. I never could. Sometimes the scene in front of us is like one of those pictures. Jesus always sees through all the squiggly and random external stuff and gets the real picture every time. The disciples didn't see it.

Maybe that's why Jesus had to take them through Samaria.

So, if you are determined to be found in the way with him, ask yourself, Who are the "Samaritans" for me, who live on the other side of my barriers of personal pride, prevailing prejudices, and unforgiving traditions? Would it be liberals, conservatives, homosexuals, AIDS victims, Baptists, Episcopalians, the homeless, prisoners, those who have offended and hurt you, weird people, mentally handicapped people, intellectuals, the uneducated? What risks would you have to take in order to engage them in a way that would allow you to bring the healing and helping love of Jesus to them? Would you risk your reputation? your money? your time? your being misunderstood or, worse, rejected? your lunch?

See what Jesus sees, and make an action plan!

Jesus cuts many new ways.

Jesus Nationals live to be found in the way with him. And the adventure has lots of interesting and sometimes challenging dimensions. But one way to follow the sound of his machete as he cuts new ways through our world is to read the Gospels and watch him walk the newly treaded landscape of life. Every time he says, "But it shall not be so among you!" or "But I say unto you," it's the sound of him cutting a whole new way.

By the end of his life on earth, MapQuest Jesus created a whole new system of roads in the Jesus Nation. For instance, in Matthew 5:43-45 Jesus says, "You have heard that it was said, 'You shall love your neighbor and hate your enemy.'" This was street talk. Like our, "I don't get mad—I get even!" He then went on to cut a new path, to welcome followers away from the heavily trafficked road of bitterness and revenge, by saying, "But I say to you, Love your enemies and pray for those who persecute you, so that you may be sons of your Father who is in heaven."

Jesus walked that way all the way to the Cross, and he looks over his shoulder and wonders if anyone is in the way with him. It's Forgiveness

Highway! And since God is a forgiving God, since he loved us even when we were his enemies, if we are followers of his we need to be found in the way with him.

He's into road building again when James and John bring their mother, Mrs. Zebedee, to ask that Jesus make her sons big shots in the new nation that he has come to birth (see Matthew 20:1-28). When the other ten heard that they had made this request, they were deeply offended. No doubt because James and John played lowball by having their mom ask the favor—but also because they all wanted it, and James and John had beaten them to the punch. So Jesus gets out the machete one more time to cut a new way, an exit from the Me-First road.

You can hear the machete when he says to them, "You know that the rulers in this world lord it over their people. . . . But among you it will be different. Whoever wants to be a leader among you must be your servant, and whoever wants to be first among you must become your slave. For even the Son of Man came not to be served but to serve others and to give his life as a ransom for many" (Matthew 20:25-28, NLT). In the Jesus Nation, the way up is down, and the road is marked Servanthood. And if you understand the choice that Jesus made to come as a servant (see Philippians 2:7) and to use his position to serve, then you know that servanthood is not a mere strategy; it's an identity. An identity that is activated regardless of our position or power—both of which can be leveraged for the benefit of others. If Jesus could hold the highest position in the universe and wield unrivaled power and use both of them to serve, then so should those of us who call ourselves followers of him.

Following parents serve the best interests of their children. Pastors serve their parishioners, and CEOs serve their employees and clients. It's why the rich serve the poor and the poor serve the rich. And *following* is why I am at Cornerstone to serve the students.

Which brings to mind another way, one that escapes a lot of people's attention. One aspect of the Jesus way that rarely shows up on theologians' lists of attributes is that he is exceedingly generous. Just look at the Cross if you doubt his generosity. And since he lived most of his life flat broke, I am particularly taken with the fact that he was generous in his spirit toward others and generous with the expenditure of his power, gifts, and talents. I guess I'm intrigued by this because I am sometimes around people who are grumpy, stingy with resources, and otherwise uptight with just about everybody and everything. In fact, I have always thought that it would be neat if God were to schedule a partial rapture of grumpy old saints so that we could get on with a more positive, mutually caring, and tolerant life in the Jesus Nation!

In John 2, we read that Jesus went to a wedding party where the wine ran out early in the celebration. This was a significant problem because Jewish wedding banquets lasted several days, unlike our three-hour ordeals in which we wait for the couple to have their pictures taken, down the food, hear some speeches, clink our glasses, and go home. So they bring the problem to Jesus. If it had been you or me, we probably would have responded with something like, "So who's the bonehead party planner who didn't get the guest count right? Don't plan on me bailing him out! He needs to learn his lesson so he won't do it to the next party." Thankfully, Jesus is not like a lot of us. Even though it wasn't his official business—"my hour has not yet come" (verse 4)—he told them to bring him water, and they brought him six jars of water holding between twenty and thirty gallons apiece. The details are important here: Do the math. Jesus is about to materialize 3,500 six-oz glasses of wine. Or as my friend Michael Card calculates, given that the host of the feast was surprised at the quality of the wine: it probably was about $36,500 worth of wine.

I call that a generous spirit.

There are lots of new paths that Jesus cuts in addition to living to prove that people matter most, living to forgive, to serve, and to give generously. Read through the Gospels and listen for the machete. As you do, choose the roads he walks on and begin the adventure of being found in the way with him.

And when you are following him, notice the times when he looks over his shoulder to see if you are there, and when he sees you, give him a thumbs-up!

113

Chapter 16

JESUS OUR CHAMPION

"SO, WHO'S YOUR FAVORITE SUPERHERO?"

The question was being asked of me by a student reporter in the first week of my presidency at Cornerstone University. It took me by surprise, given my expectations that the reporter would want to probe my vision for the school and test my scholarly inclinations. Taken off guard, since I had no clue as to who the superheroes of this high-tech video-game culture are, I feared for my survival as president. Suggesting Mighty Mouse or Flash Gordon would no doubt relegate me to ancient history and place me somewhere in the vicinity of Attila the Hun. But as the reporter stared at me expectantly I blurted out, "Superman!" Not satisfied, she asked, "Why?" I don't know how I ever came up with my answer so fast, but I said Superman was so powerful that he could leap tall buildings in a bound and at the same time carry on a nifty romance with reporter Lois Lane. Well, it saved the day. The romantic twist had captured the heart of the questioner, and we went on to weightier topics.

I'm not sure why it didn't cross my mind to say Jesus. Maybe I don't often think of him in those terms, but I should. For among all the wonderful things that he is, fewer are more life-changingly relevant than the reality that he is the ultimate superhero.

Whether it's Batman or Spider-Man, superhero stories are always the same. Against impossible odds, they are called to the rescue and with daring, self-endangering courage they defeat evil and save those who are at risk, a split second before disaster strikes. And, though it always seems that they are going to lose and be overcome by the powers of evil, they prevail. Every time!

That may just be the most exciting description of what Jesus has done for you and me when, just in the nick of time, he defeated our archenemy, Satan, who had us in his destructive grip. Like the heroine of old: tied to the tracks, with the villain in the bushes laughing in fiendish delight; helpless, hopeless, and defeated, we were unable to rescue ourselves until Jesus arrived on the scene and, at great risk to himself, with daring, self-endangering courage, grabbed us from the snarling evil one and set us free.

He fought a battle for us that we couldn't win ourselves. He is our champion!

Johnnie was a tough kid from South Hackensack, New Jersey. I had just finished eighth grade in a small Christian school, where I had reigned as Big Man on Campus. But now it was time to move on, so I went to Fairmont Junior High, a public school not far from my home—and the school Johnnie attended. Well, needless to say, my BMOC status evaporated. I was now New Kid on the Block. And Johnnie chose to prove his emerging manhood on me by pushing me around and threatening to beat me up every time I passed him in the hall or saw him on the playground.

I am sorry to say that I was traumatized. Fearing for my life, I planned how I walked home from school and how I got from one class to the other in order to avoid him. Johnnie was my archenemy. Though I had done nothing to deserve his focused hostility, he was after my hide. I begged mutual friends to come to my aid and call Johnnie off, but to no avail. I needed someone to rescue me, but no one was up to the challenge. I was up against something that was beyond me. Fear and despair were my only options. It was a tough way to start my career in public school!

In retrospect, that psyche-marring episode in my formative years was preparing me for life. It wouldn't be the first or last time that I would be up against odds that were far beyond my ability to cope. It wouldn't be the last time that I needed a champion. How often we have longed for a champion to help save our marriage, to right the wrongs that have been done to us, to bail us out of the tyranny of a creditor, to heal us from incurable cancer, to . . . well, you fill in the blank.

In ancient warfare, a certain tactic was often used to avoid massive bloodshed and loss of human life. Instead of the armies going into direct combat, each side would choose an individual as their representative to go into battle with an individual selected from the other side. Whoever would win the one-to-one engagement by killing the other combatant would in effect have won the war for his side, the enemy would be taken captive, and the spoils of victory would belong to the winning side. The conquering individual was called the champion for his nation. In fact, that is exactly the setting for the David and Goliath story in the Old Testament.

Goliath, over nine feet tall, wearing 120 pounds of armor, is taunting the quivering Israelites to send out their best man to fight against him. "He stood and shouted to the ranks of Israel, ' . . . Choose a man for yourselves, and let him come down to me. If he is able to fight with me and kill me, then we will be your servants. But if I prevail against him and kill him, then you shall be our servants and serve us'" (1 Samuel 17:8-9). No one was daring enough to take Goliath up on the offer, until the shepherd boy David stepped up to the line and, in a brave act of faith, nailed the towering giant in the forehead and struck a deathblow to the army on the other side of the valley.

David was the champion for Israel.

And just in case you are thinking that you need a David in your life—you have one. Just in the nick of time, when it looked like all was lost, Jesus went into your valley of trouble and defeated the towering giant in your life, handing him a definitive defeat, a victory you could have never won on your own. And regardless of what you are up against today or what you will be up against in the future, Jesus the champion has conquered the ultimate enemy. All the villains in life that may make you feel vulnerable and defeated are merely phantom giants bellowing their bravado on the landscape of your existence. Jesus has won! And the day is coming when all the giants will fall, at the roll of one large smooth stone that released Jesus as victor over sin and death . . . forever!

No doubt, it is this champion concept that Jesus has in mind when he morphs into quiz mode and asks the first Jesus Nationals two questions: "Who do people say that the Son of Man is?" and, "Who do you say that I am?" (Matthew 16:13, 15). The important thing to note is that these two questions are set against the backdrop of the dark side of the disciples' lives. Jesus is with his disciples in the district of Caesarea Philippi. Caesarea was named after Caesar, the despotic ruler of the oppressive empire—the empire that had taken the proud nation of Israel and put it under the heavy weight of its thumb. The Israelites lived in fear of Caesar. In order to quell the insurrectionist zealots in Israel, thousands of Jews had been crucified by Philip the tetrarch's father, Herod the Great, on behalf of Caesar, in order to keep the restless outpost under control.

Being in Caesarea Philippi reeked of all that the disciples feared and despised.

Not only was it a place of honor to their enemies, but it was also a place in which idolatry was rampant. Though the town held a large temple to the god Zeus, its preeminent god was Pan. This was the Vatican of Pan followers. Pan was the god of fertility, half goat and half man. Bestiality was committed with goats as a part of their worship and most likely was practiced in the open courts of Pan's temple. The opening of a deep cave that descended into the earth, known as the gates of Hades, was a part of his temple. According to their mythology, Pan would descend into the cave, into the presence of hell, and emerge again after winter with his semen, symbolizing the new birth of spring. The worship was so frenzied that we get our words *panic* and *pandemonium* from these scenes. Today if you go to that part of the world, there's a city named Banias, after the god Pan that was once worshiped there.

So not only did the disciples have the repulsive symbols of the empire to deal with, but they also had the blatant and decadent pagan idolatry that would have offended even the most callous Jewish soul. Just speaking the name *Caesarea Philippi* made Jewish blood run cold.

It's important to remind ourselves here that when Jesus asked questions, he didn't ask them because he didn't know the answer. He asked questions constantly to stimulate thought processes, to prod the disciples (and us) more deeply. Remember when you would walk into your house for dinner and your mother would say, "Did you wash your hands?" She knew good and well you hadn't washed your hands; she wanted you to start examining yourself and do something about it. That's what Jesus is after here.

We should also note that he is not asking these questions because he is feeling insecure about his "press." He's just out of a pretty serious food fight with the Pharisees and the Sadducees in the beginning of the chapter, and maybe coming out of that he's thinking, "How am I doing? Does anyone know who I am? Tell me . . ."

Not Jesus. He knows who he is and how he is doing, and he's never concerned about his public image. He's asking these questions to get his followers to engage with who he really is in the face of our most dreaded moments in life.

The first question is a lobbed ball: "Who do people say that I am?"

They've been reading the headlines and hearing the local chatter, so they repeat what they have heard. They reply, "Some say John the Baptist, some say Elijah, and others say Jeremiah or one of the other prophets" (Matthew 16:14, NLT). There is an important historical context here. The tradition among the Jews was that the sign of the coming Messiah would be Elijah's coming back. In fact, even today in Orthodox Judaism, when the Feast of the Passover is celebrated, there is an empty chair at every celebration of the Passover for Elijah with the hope that he will come as a forerunner of the imminent Messianic arrival. So for the disciples, this is easy answer time. Nothing personally penetrating, just the facts. Report time. That was the easy part of the quiz.

It's the follow-up question that puts our brains up against the wall. Jesus asks, "Who do you say that I am?" In Greek, the personal pronouns are emphasized. It's like he looks them right in the eye and says, "Who do *you* say that I am?" My guess is that none of the disciples wanted to be quick with this answer. If Jesus asks you, "Who do you say that I am?" you don't want to be wrong. I can almost see the disciples putting their hands to their chins and bowing their heads with thoughtful looks in their eyes, scratching the toes of their sandals in the dirt and hoping one of the others will be the first to venture an answer. So who do you need at a time like this? Peter, of course! And he doesn't let us down. With apparently fearless confidence, he blurts out, "You are the Christ, the Son of the living God" (Matthew 16:16).

If you ever watched the TV quiz show *Who Wants to Be a Millionaire*, you remember how, when an answer was given to a high-stakes question, the host would wait for a few seconds to raise the suspense before saying, "You are right, and you've just won a million dollars!" I'd like to think that there was a pause here when all the disciples, including Peter, were locked in suspense about the outcome of this high-stakes question. Regardless, you can be sure that Peter breathed a sigh of relief when Jesus affirmed that he had gotten it precisely right!

And he did have it right. In an important follow-up, Jesus told Peter three things. First, you are blessed for knowing and believing that I am the Christ; second, this is the kind of information that only comes when God reveals it to you; and third, what you have just said is the very foundation for the church and for its power against the gates of hell (see Matthew 16:17-18).

By the way, I wonder what your answer would have been as you stood there moving your sandal back and forth in the sand, trying to reflect on all the possibilities. Creator, Savior, Friend? There'd be a lot of good answers. But there's only one right answer at the top of the list.

He is the Christ.

The word *Christ* is the New Testament word for "Messiah." The Messiah was seen by the Jews as that one who would come and be the final deliverer from all the oppression and humiliation that they had suffered for hundreds of years.

When the prophets spoke of the Messiah, they rolled three Jewish personalities into their hope in the Messiah: prophet, priest, and king. So in Peter's mind, Jesus was a prophet, a priest, and a king. Prophets spoke for God; they brought God's Word to God's people. Priests made a way for people to connect to God and to find both forgiveness and fellowship with their Creator. Kings conquered the enemies of God and kept God's people safe. So when Peter said, "You are the Christ," he was affirming that Jesus would bring God's Word, make a way for us to get to God, and defeat our enemies for us and keep us safe.

And so, this declaration by Peter, made against the dazzling backdrop of the temple built by Herod to the glory of Caesar and the pagan temple of Pan, holds within its articulation all the hopes and dreams of a weary and fearful nation. They were looking for a new nation. A nation that Jesus would usher in as conquering king.

For getting an A+ on the quiz, Peter seems to get a prize. Jesus replies, "Blessed are you Simon Bar-Jonah! For flesh and blood has not revealed this to you, but my Father who is in heaven. And I tell you, you are Peter, and on this rock I will build my church, and the gates of hell shall not prevail against it. I will give you the keys of the kingdom of heaven, and whatever you bind on earth shall be bound in heaven, and whatever you loose on earth shall be loosed in heaven" (Matthew 16:17-19).

Peter's prize has been the center of controversy in the church for centuries. What did Jesus mean when he said, "On this rock I will build my church"? Was that the first time we saw white smoke rising to announce a pope? For many reasons that are not necessary to list now, probably not. I can't imagine the other disciples saying, "Shoot, I wanted the cool hat and the glass limo!"

Then what is Jesus getting at? For all the theories that try to untangle this statement, one thing is true. The declaration that "Jesus is the Christ," the ultimate conqueror and champion, is the rock-solid foundation that the church has been built on and placed its hope in. And it is the one central truth that the gates of hell cannot defend against! While it is true that *Peter* means stone, it is also true that the word Matthew uses for the rock upon which the church is built is *bedrock*. It references the huge plates of rock that undergird the earth. That's a perfect image for what the conquering work of Jesus does for the church.

But—and this is a very important consideration—Peter's expectation was all out of whack. He thought that Jesus would be a political, sociological, and religious revolutionary who would cure all of Peter's anxieties and put his life in a good place. Sound familiar? There are more than a few of us who had hoped that Jesus would chase away the troublemakers in our life and set us up on easy street. And then there's the twisted talk on religious TV that offers us wealth, health, and happiness if we have enough faith and put a modest offering in the mail to the "evangelist."

Wrong.

Wrong then; wrong now.

Certainly Jesus will give us grace to cope (see 2 Corinthians 12:9), see that nothing happens to us that we cannot bear (see 1 Corinthians 10:13), turn the tables on the enemy by ensuring that all things ultimately work together for good (see Romans 8:28), and eventually airlift us out forever to a much better place (see John 14:1-4).

But for now, Jesus is not about feathering our nest. He is hell-bent, you might say, on finalizing the death sentence on the real culprit: hell itself! Matthew recalls, "From that time Jesus began to show his disciples that he must go to Jerusalem and suffer many things from the elders and chief priests and scribes, and be killed, and on the third day be raised." From Peter's perspective, this is crazy talk. How can you be the Christ and get yourself killed? So, Peter "took him aside and began to rebuke him, saying, 'Far be it from you, Lord! This shall never happen to you.'" Poor Peter. He goes from an A+ to an F within seven verses! Peter's error prompted an abrupt reproof from Jesus: "Get behind me, Satan! You are a hindrance to me. For you are not setting your mind on the things of God, but on the things of man" (Matthew 16:21-23).

Ever wonder why Jesus called Peter "Satan"? It's because it had a familiar ring to Jesus: Peter's whisper is exactly the temptation that Satan offered Jesus in the wilderness. Only the voices had changed. Satan had taken Jesus to the pinnacle of the Temple and offered him the kingdoms and the riches of this world. *Just bow down and worship me, and you can bypass the Cross. I'll let you be king of everything.* Peter's suggestion reminded Jesus of that moment when Satan offered him a shortcut around suffering to immediate gratification.

But Jesus would not be sidetracked by Satan, Peter, or anyone else. Jesus knew that he didn't come to deal with the symptoms; he came to conquer the problem. And there's a huge difference between the two.

Sure, Jesus could have made it so that his followers would never face hardship and that only the righteous would prosper. He could put their enemies in the ditch and send Rome running with a wink and a nod. But the devilish mastermind behind all those things would have come up with some new scheme. It wasn't the torchlit army in the garden that Peter wanted to take on by de-earing the frontline lieutenant that posed the threat. It was the general who was behind it all. And not the one in Rome.

It was going to be a huge fight, and it was going to look like Jesus was a real loser before it was all done.

So Jesus told his disciples that soon he would enter into the arena face-to-face with Satan and he would do battle on an old rugged cross with bloodstained timbers. He would go against the enemy of our souls. He would go to the depths of hell and fight the battle on our behalf and win. And we would share in the spoils.

Our champion!

And so he died. And the disciples felt defeated, afraid, and ready to bail. Imagine the party in hell! Three days of music, reveling, and dancing! And bloody old Beelzebub, gloating on his throne. We won! Show the video again . . . And then on the third day some minion demon whispered in Beelzebub's ear, "I've got some bad news, some really bad news. He's alive; he beat you head-to-head. We're finished!"

When the enemy of your soul fills your heart with despair, remember this: Jesus has already won! Satan has been dealt the ultimate deathblow. Don't let the stench of his dying corpse defeat you. Jesus has defeated the primary source of your turmoil. Don't let the symptoms get you down!

J. R. R. Tolkien, brilliant author of the Lord of the Rings trilogy, wrote in its opening chapters about little plump hobbits who lived in Middle-earth happy and undisturbed. Until the Dark Riders entered the scene and the ring of power and evil was discovered. For Tolkien, it was more than a mere fantasy birthed out of his clever imagination. When he was four, his father died. By the time he was twelve, his mother had died as well. By the end of the First World War, all of his friends but one had been killed. Is it any wonder that he wrote a story about vulnerable little hobbits, going about their merry way, suddenly invaded by the powers of evil, in the face of which the hobbits cannot help themselves and are left totally vulnerable?

It is why Frodo said to a friend when the Dark Riders appeared, "I knew there was danger way down the road but I never thought I'd see danger in my homeland."[1]

In a sense, we are all hobbits. We are up against the ultimate enemy—the ultimate Dark Rider—and without a champion, we have no hope.[2]

A friend of mine who was in the middle of an extremely successful career went to the doctor's office for routine testing that revealed he had life-threatening thyroid cancer and would have to undergo a surgery that could be life threatening. As he was lying on the gurney, having kissed his family good-bye, he later told me, "For the first time in my life all of my success, everything I had done meant nothing."

That's hobbit talk. He was now left alone to battle something far beyond his capacity to conquer. "I lay there and started thinking that I was facing death all by myself," he said. "Then I remembered that I wasn't all by myself, that Jesus had already faced death for me, that Christ had already conquered death. In my soul it was like peace and joy were bursting forth! Death can come and get me if it wants, but I'm just going on to someplace better because Jesus is my Christ. My Conquering One!" He went on to say, "Just to know that death had no sting, that the grave had no victory, was a great gift to me in that moment. I was rolled in and went under the anesthetic with an unbelievable sense of joy and peace."

So, what was his answer to the pop quiz? For him, too, Jesus is the Christ, and he knew exactly what that meant. There are some situations you just can't lick on your own. It's then that you know that you are not the champion and that without help you will be a loser, big-time. So when those times come, remember that you have a champion. And that champion is Jesus.

It reminds me of the book of Revelation, where mortal man is faced with odds of supernatural proportion, yet Jesus is the undisputed champion.

My all-time favorite story of the ultimate outcome of the book of Revelation is about a stuffy theology professor who was walking through the seminary basement on his lunch hour and saw a custodian reading his Bible as he ate his sandwich from an open lunch box. Stopping to ask the custodian what he was reading, he was surprised to hear the janitor say, "Revelation." "I don't suppose you know what it all means" was the condescending response of the theologian. The lunching sanitary engineer said, "Actually, I do!" Shocked, the professor replied, "Really! What does it mean?" To which the confident custodian replied, "Jesus wins!"

I was teaching the letters to the seven churches found in Revelation 1–3 on a cruise and tour of the ancient sites of those early Christian outposts. In the process of explaining the overview of Revelation, I told that same story. As our cruise ship anchored in the harbor of the Isle of Patmos, we all disembarked to tour the island and to see the cave where John is supposed to have received the words that he wrote in Revelation. Upon reboarding, one of the passengers proudly told us that she was shopping in a jewelry store and saw a pendant with an ancient cross that had the letters IC XC NIKA written in the quadrants of the cross. When she asked the shopkeeper what the inscription meant, he replied, "Jesus wins!" The passenger went on to explain that the letters stood for "Jesus Christ the Victor," which was the slogan of the early church after the Roman emperor Constantine converted to Christianity and declared it the religion of the empire. Needless to say, her find sparked a flurry of shopping by the rest of the group, who descended on every jewelry store at every stop on the tour to find the conquering symbol of the early church for their own collection.

You can imagine how delighted I was when on my sixtieth birthday my kids gave me a ring with the victory symbol engraved in the quadrants of a cross. I wear it every day to remind myself that regardless of what I am up against, in the end, Jesus wins. He is my champion, and I belong to a nation that will never be defeated.

A friend of mine showed me his World Series championship ring. It was huge, impressive, and clearly carried legitimate bragging rights. I didn't tell him that I was wearing a championship ring as well. It seemed like a bad case of one-upmanship to tell him that his championship only lasted until next season, whereas I was wearing the "Jesus wins forever" championship ring.

When the writer of Hebrews says that Jesus is "the author and finisher of our faith" (Hebrews 12:2, KJV), he uses the Greek words for "arch-ego," or "ultimate man." Jesus is our main man, our champion. It's no wonder that the writer exclaims, "It was fitting that he, for whom and by whom all things exist, in bringing many sons to glory, should make the founder of their salvation perfect through suffering. . . . Since therefore the children share in flesh and blood, he himself likewise partook of the same things, that through death he might destroy the one who has the power of death, that is, the devil, and deliver all those who through fear of death were subject to lifelong slavery" (Hebrews 2:10, 14-15).

It's no wonder that Paul—who had been imprisoned, shipwrecked, beaten, and disliked by many—wrote, "We are afflicted in every way, but not crushed; perplexed, but not driven to despair; persecuted, but not forsaken; struck down, but not destroyed" (2 Corinthians 4:8-9). And in Romans 8:31-34, he displays the unflagging confidence he has in Jesus as his champion when he writes, "What then shall we say to these things? If God is for us, who can be against us? He who did not spare his own Son but gave him up for us all, how will he not also with him graciously give us all things? Who shall bring any charge against God's elect? . . . Christ Jesus is the one who died—more than that, who was raised—who is at the right hand of God, who indeed is interceding for us." And then Paul concludes:

> Who shall separate us from the love of Christ? Shall tribulation, or distress, or persecution, or famine, or nakedness, or danger, or sword? . . . No, in all these things we are more than conquerors through him who loved us. For I am sure that neither death nor life, nor angels nor rulers, nor things present nor things to come, nor powers, nor height nor depth, nor anything else in all creation, will be able to separate us from the love of God in Christ Jesus our Lord. (Romans 8:35, 37-39)

Just over a month after Bill became a believer, his wife Erin had a massive internal hemorrhage and almost died. The doctors brought her back to life again three times that night. Since then, she has had two additional hemorrhages, both of which almost killed her as well, and two additional major surgeries. The doctors accidentally punctured a lung during the chaos, and she has been on a tracheal tube for much of the ordeal. Her vocal chords were damaged because of the breathing tube, and now she can barely speak. At one point, when it looked like she was on the road to recovery, she began to bleed internally again—leading to another surgery, leading to a life-threatening infection.

Erin had been in the hospital for seventy-two days when I heard about her tragic story. During this time, Bill nearly lost his job and had been forced to use up all of his vacation and personal time. He basically lived at the hospital. This would be enough to sink even a seasoned believer, yet remarkably Bill's newfound confidence in God was unshaken.

Bill wrote this note to his small-group leader:

> The last five months have been totally life changing for me and Erin. I agree with you wholeheartedly that no one knows God's plan. The only thing I can say is, once you realize he is in control all you can do is trust in God and let him lead you. It's not a good plan to resist, fight, or ignore him. I believe I allowed the Holy Spirit to guide me (although sometimes he needed to really bang me on the head), and I just knew deep down inside that God was going to take care of us during this season. It has been God who has given me the strength and wisdom to get through this time. I don't know what the future holds for Erin and me, so all we can do is pray that good things will continue to happen as we continue to grow in our faith. When you place yourself totally in God's care, he will get you through. It may not be in the way that you want him to, but in the end he will get you through.

A friend of Bill's wrote me, "Bill's confidence in God is unshakable!"

Bill hadn't been in the Jesus Nation long, but he learned early on that he had a champion, a superhero, who had already defeated the demonic onslaught. That he belonged to a nation that was the assured winner. That the sickness, though tragically real, was only a vaporous stench from hell that would soon be replaced by the sweet aroma of our champion's victory.

And this is why Jesus Nationals are confidently courageous, regardless.

Part 4

BECOMING TRUE JESUS NATIONALS

◆

GENEROSITY, GRACE, AND GLORY

Chapter 17

BARN BUILDERS BEWARE

IF YOU THINK IT IS STRANGE that I would choose to do a section about money in a book about living in the Jesus Nation, it may not be as strange as you think, particularly when you realize that Jesus taught more about money than any other topic. And what I find fascinating is that, as far as we know, he never took an offering.

So he wasn't teaching about money in order to get everybody on board with the new capital campaign. He taught frequently about money because he knew that nothing clogs our spiritual arteries more quickly than having a lot of money, making it our goal to make a lot of money, sitting around ticked that someone else made a lot of money, or just wishing that we had a lot of money. Money is a major culprit in laying out life-tangling nets that hold the best of us back from following Jesus.

Jesus has a national economy, and like everything else in his nation, what he tells us about money is really counterintuitive—revolutionary, in fact. So cash in all your past thoughts about how cool it would be to have a lot of it, and let's let Jesus put on his financial adviser hat. Nowhere is he clearer about the "upside-down toastness" of thinking wrongly about money than he is in Luke 12:13 and following.

I love this story. But you have to put yourself in the crowd that watches it all unfold to appreciate what Jesus wants to say to you. Remember that Jesus at this point was the magnet-like rabbi of his day. Everyplace he went, people flocked to him. Everyone wanted a piece of him, to have his personal attention. And if you got his attention, you would want him to sign your Torah.

That makes what happens in this text amazing.

A gentleman in the crowd locks eyes with Jesus. Big moment. Big opportunity to interact with the headliner of his day. You'd think that he would want to go deep with Jesus. Think again.

Luke tells us that "someone in the crowd said to him, 'Teacher, tell my brother to divide the inheritance with me'" (Luke 12:13). My feeling is that if you get one shot at Jesus, that is probably not the right thing to say.

If I had one shot at a personal interaction with Jesus, I'd like to say something so profound that Jesus would say, "Hmm, I never thought of that. Could we have dinner and discuss your interesting point?"

An opportunity to go deep with Jesus, and all the guy wanted was for Jesus to line his pockets. It's not unlike the fantasy we indulge ourselves in when we give our tithes, believing that he will reward us with more money. Or that joining the right church or small group will be good for business contacts. Or that giving a mere 10 percent will earn a guilt-free ride on excursions to Stuffville and Pilestown.

So, Jesus turns to the crowd. The revolutionary is about to speak. No doubt everyone who heard the request for fairness in Money World was wondering how Jesus would adjudicate this family feud. There were rabbinical laws about such things, so you might expect that Jesus would come down hard on a brother who had kept all the goods for himself. It actually seemed like a safe question, and one with a point. But Jesus knew that the real culprit was not the hoarding brother but something far deeper that lurked in the heart of everyone who was now all ears to hear Christ's answer.

Greed.

In typical Jesus fashion, he goes after the disease, not the symptom. And he does it by making a stunning observation. It's one that no doubt has rarely crossed your mind: "Take care, and be on your guard against all covetousness, for one's life does not consist in the abundance of his possessions" (Luke 12:15). Press the Pause button. You've got to freeze-frame this proposition. There isn't a fully dressed person in his right mind who would have dared to say that. Not in our he-who-dies-with-the-most-toys-wins world. As we have noted, most of us flip Paul's formula and live as though he said, "For me, to live is gain, and to die is Christ" (see

Philippians 1:21). Or, to turn another one of Paul's formulas upside down, we live as though "godliness with gain is great contentment" (see 1 Timothy 6:6, NIV). Since the first Christmas when we were old enough to unwrap a gift, we started thinking that life was about getting what we wanted. And it was clear that this notion of it being all about the goodies was deeply embedded in our psyches when we became depressed about getting socks and underwear for Christmas. Obviously, we need help.

THE DANGER ZONE OF GREED

For starters, Jesus puts a warning label on this package. He says, "Take care, and be on your guard against all covetousness" (Luke 12:15). Or literally, as the Greek says, "Beware." Anytime Jesus says "beware," it means you're in a lot of danger. Or as you and I might put it, "Look out!" Greed—or covetousness, as it's called in this story—is a yellow-taped danger zone.

If it's that dangerous, we need to look closely so that we can understand the problem. The Greek word for greed and covetousness literally means "more." It's the insatiable disease that wants more when we already have more. It's the way you feel when you finally buy that thirty-foot boat you've been dreaming about. And, as you are sitting on the stern deck sipping lemonade in your nifty slip at the marina, Bob pulls up in the slip next to yours in his brand-new thirty-five-foot boat. And in your heart you are saying to yourself, *I should've bought that forty-foot boat!*

Several years ago, Martie and I moved out of Chicago to the western suburbs to be near our grandkids. We got this little piece of land and built what we thought was our dream house. It was not over the top by any means, but it was nice. We liked how it looked from the curb. We liked how it lived on the inside. It was far more than we deserved, but we really liked our house. I hate to admit this to you, but about six months after we built our house, I was driving through a beautiful neighborhood and saw a house that caught my attention. The colors, the architecture, the lot, the location all had a big wow factor for me. And my first thought was, *Boy, do I wish I had that house!*

Have you ever wondered, *What is wrong with us?* It's the Eve factor in our lives. We were born with it, and it's deeply embedded in our spiritual DNA. Just one more proof of our sinfulness, in case we had forgotten.

What was it that drew Eve's heart away from God in Genesis 3? What was it that seduced her into the material world, into Satan's clutches? She wanted more. What she had, although absolutely awesome and satisfying, wasn't enough.

In fact, for her, God wasn't enough. She was willing to do anything for more, even if it meant turning her back on God. At its core, greed is a lack of contentment with God and with what he has provided for us. No wonder the problem of covetousness made the Big Ten in the Old Testament. And in the New Testament, Paul says that greed is idolatry—pretty serious charge—and that we are to put it to death (see Colossians 3:5).

Warning us about the danger of greed, Jesus goes on to tell us why living for "more" is a futile pursuit. "For one's life does not consist in the abundance of his possessions" (Luke 12:15). Talk about counterintuitive! Our whole world runs on the premise that life consists in our accumulation of things, that the abundance of our possessions is directly related to the abundance of our happiness. Jesus warns us about this kind of thinking.

THE GOOD LIFE

A few years ago, the banking empire Citicorp ran a series of billboard ads that were surprisingly not very financial. In my mind, banks want you to make money so you can give it to them and they can make more money while offering you an interest bonus for the privilege. These ads suggested that Citicorp wanted you to think differently about your money. Whether that's actually true or not, I enjoyed the different perspective.

The ads were usually large black letters on a white background. They were hard to miss:

- "People make money. Not the other way around."
- "Miser is only four letters shy of miserable."
- "He who dies with the most toys is still dead."
- "The people you work for are waiting for you at home right now."
- "If you keep your nose to the grindstone, you'll look funny."
- "If people describe you as made of money, you should work on your personality."
- "Today's must-have is often tomorrow's what-was-I-thinking?"

- "Some of the most exciting growth charts are on the back of the pantry door."

Brilliant and counterintuitive, the ads helped us to get a grip on what life is *not* about. But my all-time favorite story about the essence of life is this one.

A young investment banker stood looking out into the cool gulf waters before him on the end of a pier in a small coastal Mexican village. Having spent the last several months working hard toward gaining his securities license, he had taken a few days of sun-soaked pleasure.

As the golden sun sank into the horizon, a single fisherman docked his boat along the far side of the pier. The young banker complimented the wise-eyed, weathered fisherman on the quality of his fish and asked how long it took him to bring in the catch.

"Not long," said the fisherman.

The young banker said, "Why not stay out longer and catch more fish?"

"I have enough for today."

"What do you do with the rest of your time?" the banker asked.

"I sleep late, fish a little, play with my children, take a siesta with my wife, Maria, and stroll into the village each evening, where I enjoy some wine and laughter with my friends. It's a full and happy life," the fisherman said.

"Well, I'm an MBA from Harvard; I could help you," said the banker. "You could spend more time fishing, and with the proceeds from the larger catch, buy a bigger boat. Then you could catch more fish, and with these profits you could buy several more boats and hire captains to fish for you. Eventually, you could open your own cannery. Then you could control the product, processing, and distribution. Of course, you would need to leave this small coastal village and move to Mexico City or L.A. or New York or somewhere, where you could run your expanding enterprise."

The fisherman asked, "How long would that take?"

"Just fifteen years, maybe twenty, max."

"But what then?" asked the fisherman.

"Well, when the time is right you could announce your IPO, sell your company's stock to the public, and become very rich. You could be worth millions."

"Millions? Then what?"

"Well, then you could retire, move to a small coastal village like this one—where you could sleep late, fish a little in the morning, play with your grandchildren, take a siesta with Maria, and enjoy wine with your friends in the evening."

Driving down the interstate in Houston a few summers ago, I noticed a billboard in the distance that said, "The Good Life" in huge letters. I couldn't wait to see the fine print. When I got closer it said, "Lakefront houses $450,000 and up." And I said to myself, *I don't think so.* Although not every family who can afford such luxury has their priorities off, what about all the dual-career couples who are working hard to make the mortgage payments and leaving latchkey kids at home? What about those who hoped property would satisfy their souls and heal their relationships, but who are fighting it out all the time, living on the edge of divorce, in those kinds of homes? What about those whose excessive mortgage payments put their lives under strain and duress?

Especially in these economic times, we know that lakefront houses starting at $450,000 do not guarantee "the good life." In fact, when we think of the good life as being offered by commodities, we are already out of balance—and the rest of our lives is ready to follow suit.

This kind of wrongheaded thinking is nothing new. In fact, to help free us from that particular bondage, Jesus told a story about it.

> The land of a rich man produced plentifully, and he thought to himself, "What shall I do, for I have nowhere to store my crops?" And he said, "I will do this: I will tear down my barns and build larger ones, and there I will store all my grain and my goods. And I will say to my soul, Soul, you have ample goods laid up for many years; relax, eat, drink, be merry." (Luke 12:16-19)

But before we rush to crown him Businessman of the Year, keep reading. As Luke reports, Jesus went on to say that God showed up unexpectedly and called the rich man a fool—which, to anyone listening to this story, was a revolutionary, counterintuitive thought. Nobody in his village would have thought that man a fool. He was the local success story. The Warren Buffett of his neck of the woods. *If only he would write a book,* How to Get Rich Like Me, they would have thought, *we could all be rollin' in the dough!* But God rips off the faux glory of gain by asking him a penetrating question: "Fool! This night your soul is required of you, and the things you have prepared, whose will they be?" (Luke 12:20).

Have you ever seen a Brink's truck following a hearse? Let's keep in mind that everything gets checked at the border. And, it needs to be noted, God calls him a fool not because he has a lot of money, but rather because is not rich *toward God.* As Jesus summarized, "So is the one who lays up treasure for himself and is not rich toward God" (Luke 12:21).

When God thinks about whether or not you are rich, he never measures it by your bank account. God has a whole other definition of what it means to be truly rich. In God's eyes, you can be very wealthy in this world's goods and yet be in dire poverty in your soul. Or you could be poor in terms of earthside stuff and be lavishly rich by God's standards.

Getting this straight is all about definitions. A Texas rancher who was consulting in Germany said to the German farmer, "How big is your farm?" The German's response was, "Not all that big. It's about a mile this way and about a half mile the other way." Then the German farmer asked the Texan, "How big is your ranch?" The rancher said, "I don't know how to tell you this, but if I start in my pickup truck in the morning when the sun's coming up and I drive all day long, when the sun goes down, I'm still on my ranch." The German replied, "I used to have a pickup truck like that, myself."

Life is about getting the definitions right. Particularly when it comes to money and the economy of the Jesus Nation. So what does it mean to become rich toward God? The story gives us four steps. Let's look at them.

Chapter 18

BECOMING RICH TOWARD GOD

STEP 1

Pursue Jesus as the true source of satisfaction and fulfillment.
Note that the man in the crowd had an opportunity to have Jesus give him soul wealth, but he couldn't resist the pull of personal gain in trying to get Jesus to settle a money argument with his brother.

I think of the story of the rich man who came to Jesus (see Mark 10:17-22). After a conversation about eternal life and the law, Jesus asks him to sell all he has, give to the poor, and follow him. Mark tells us that Jesus loved him, but the rich man "was disheartened by the saying" and "went away sorrowful" (Mark 10:17-22). Jesus was not against his wealth. But the tension that Jesus put on the wealthy man points to a larger question, What is of greater value? Following Jesus, or retaining wealth?

One thing is clear: You can't serve Christ and riches at the same time. As Jesus said, you can only serve one master (see Matthew 6:24). Of course you can be smart, work hard, and make a lot of money in your lifetime. But if it's the main pursuit of your life, then Jesus isn't. Jesus doesn't share space with stuff. And, as a follower of him, you may come to a point in your life when Jesus asks for your earthside wealth. What then? If money is your idol, then you will live for it and not for God. But if Jesus has become the source of satisfaction and fulfillment for you, then money is merely secondary.

The fact that the rich young ruler bailed on Jesus only goes to prove the power of the pull of affluence. It reminds me of the warning God gave the Israelites about the capacity of the accumulation of wealth to eclipse their need for God. As they stand ready to occupy the land that will be flowing with milk and honey, he says, "When the LORD your God brings you into the land that he swore to your fathers . . . with great and good cities that you did not build, and houses full of all good things that you did not fill, and cisterns that you did not dig, and vineyards and olive trees that you did not plant—and when you eat and are full, then take care lest you forget the LORD" (Deuteronomy 6:10-12).

Here's a warning label to plaster across your heart. Beware: The gifts of wealth that Jesus has given you can easily eclipse your need for the giver himself. It's like trading gold for plastic. For none of us will know true riches until we make Jesus the pursuit of our hearts, the source of ultimate joy and satisfaction. Live to go deep with Jesus, who "though he was rich, yet for your sake he became poor, so that you by his poverty might become rich" (2 Corinthians 8:9).

STEP 2

Live gratefully by acknowledging God as the ultimate source of your wealth.

When Jesus tells the story about the rich fool to the crowd, he says in the parable, "The land of a rich man produced plentifully" (see Luke 12:16). Note that Jesus attributes the abundant wealth of this farmer to "the land."

Remember that Jesus told this story in a day when they didn't have genetically engineered hybrid seeds. There were no irrigation sprinklers that swept the field to keep the moisture content on target. No nifty chemicals that are time released to ensure that the nutrients are evenly distributed. For this farmer, a great harvest was totally dependent on God's blessing and provision of rain, sun, wind, and season. Notice that Jesus did not say this rich man was so clever that he had a great harvest. God had prospered the land, and the land had made him rich. This is a point that should not get lost on us.

It's easy to think that our wealth is the direct product of how clever we are. But the reality is that you would have nothing if God had not given you the brain you have. You would have nothing if God did not wire you to be the cleverest person in your office. You would be nothing if for some reason you didn't grow up in an environment that enabled you to be a risk taker. You would be nothing if God hadn't enabled you to get the education that you've had and put you in places where doors open up in front of you that don't open up for anybody else. You are what you are and you have what you have by the abundant, unbelievable grace of God on your behalf.

But if you're patting yourself on the back, then you remind me of Little Jack Horner. The nursery rhyme says that Little Jack Horner sat in the corner eating his Christmas pie; he put in his thumb and pulled out a plum and said, "What a good boy am I." But I have to ask, if he is such a good boy, what's he doing sitting in the corner? And if I remember correctly from Nursery-Rhyme World, he's sitting with a full pie on his lap. I've never seen a mother give a boy a full pie. So no doubt he has stolen that pie from the kitchen. And what's he doing with his fingers in the food? Yet he has the audacity to claim glory for himself because he's found a plum that his mother put in the pie. If he really were a good boy, he'd have the decency to say, "Look at this wonderful plum. My mom went out early this morning, shopping for the best plums, and made this great pie. Let's hear it for my mom!" But he can't resist taking the credit for something he didn't do. His pride is in full gear, and his gratitude is in the ditch.

When you start taking the credit God deserves, you are in a bad place. King Nebuchadnezzar did that, and God sent him out to the field like an animal to eat grass for seven years (see Daniel 4:28-33). Remember where your wealth comes from. We have what we have because God has given us all we have. He is the one who fills your cup to overflowing (see Psalm 23:5). He is the one who kills the fatted calf and gives the best robe (see Luke 15:11-24). He is the one who does "exceedingly abundantly above all that we ask or think" (Ephesians 3:20, KJV). He is the one who poured out generous mercy and grace at the Cross for us.

And when he has been generous to us in giving us our wealth and an ample supply of stuff to support and entertain us, it should strike a spirit of humble gratitude in our hearts. And that's a much happier way to live than with the toxic air of pride in our spirit.

It can't escape our notice that the rich fool uses the personal pronoun referencing his riches, his plans, and his party fourteen times in this brief story (Luke 12:17-19). Not once does he tip his hat to the fact that there may have been other forces at work that gave him the abundant harvest. And all the while it wasn't about him at all.

STEP 3

Build your legacy carefully.

For two thousand years we have dubbed this story as that of the "rich fool." So that's his legacy. Quite frankly, that's not a legacy I want to have. All of us are building legacies in our lives. And at some point we have to ask, "What do I want to be remembered for?" What do you want to have your kids say about you? What do you want to have your grandkids tell their kids about you? What kind of a legacy do you want?

So here are some choices: my dad was always at the office . . . my parents always had really cool cars . . . my parents always worried about money and how they were going to pay off their credit card bills . . . my parents never seemed to care much about the appeals from missionaries for help in the work . . . my parents always had a lot of neat things, but I had to pay for my own college bills . . . my parents lived in a great house and had really nice things, so I want to be sure I can live like that as well.

Or, would you want your legacy to sound like this? "One thing I've learned from my grandfather is how important it is to be generous. . . . My dad was a man of unflinching integrity, and I remember when he said no to some pretty lucrative opportunities because it would have taken him away from us and from his commitment to God's work through our church. . . . My grandmother didn't have a lot, but I remember how she loved hospitality, and if someone had a need, she was right there to help."

Your life is building memories that will be formative in generations to come. Build your legacy carefully!

STEP 4

Draw the line at enough, and give the rest away.

The story says that the rich fool asks himself, "'What shall I do, for I have nowhere to store my crops?' And he said, 'I will do this: I will tear down my barns and build larger ones, and there I will store all my grain and my goods'" (Luke 12:17-18).

It strikes me that he already had enough. If his barns were already full and if as Jesus says he was already a rich man before the harvest, why did he need to build more barns? I find myself wondering if it ever crossed his mind that maybe there were some poor people in his town who could have been blessed with his wealth. What about the poor farmer down the road who for some reason didn't have all that great a harvest but had a lot of mouths to feed? Or did his village need a new hospital?

It's clear that it never crosses his mind that he could be a blessing with his wealth. All he could hear were the cheerleaders in his heart chanting, "Build more barns! Build more barns! Build more barns!"

I wonder if you have ever considered drawing a line at enough and giving the rest away?

When I drive north from Grand Rapids, there is a huge garbage mountain with pipes that let the gases escape from the tens of thousands of tons of stuff that has been thrown away. The smell is almost unbearable. It makes me think of all the things buried there that offered to be the end all of end alls in some flashy store at the mall. But when you decide that generosity and contentment will replace greed and covetousness in your heart, and you start giving things away, the joy you thought you'd get from hoarding comes when you become generous and give to needs and to others who are in need.

So, how do you know when you have enough? I can't tell you that. There's no cookie-cutter formula for all of us. But my guess is that enough is far less than you think it needs to be.

Early in our marriage, we got some great advice. With too much month left at the end of the money, we were struggling to make ends meet. So a wise mentor challenged us to first double our giving to things that counted for eternity; to structure a plan to get out of debt; and then to stop charging and pay cash, trusting God to supply for our needs. It seemed radical and, humanly speaking, impossible. But it worked—and I've lived long enough to tell you that it has been a delight. We find far more joy in giving than in buying. No wonder we read that it's better to give than to receive (see Acts 20:35).

And this idea doesn't necessarily mean that you can't go out to dinner on Friday nights or get that new fishing rod. For some of us, even a new flat-screen TV isn't out of the question. As 1 Timothy 6:17 says, "God

. . . richly provides us with everything to enjoy." But it is important to note that the next verse says that those who are rich should be rich in good works; they should be generous, willing to share, not conceited, and not putting their hope and trust in the uncertainty of riches.

Chapter 19

PROSPERITY IN PERSPECTIVE

NOW THAT WE HAVE transitioned to greed-free living, Jesus moves us to the joy of generosity or, as he puts it, becoming rich toward God. But it won't come easily. The anxiety for having enough will threaten to paralyze us unless we let Jesus teach us something about our Father in heaven.

When Jesus wraps up the story of the rich fool, he turns from addressing the crowd to challenge his disciples. This is an important transition in the text. He starts with the man who asked the question about his inheritance, he works the crowd with the story of the rich fool, and then he finally turns to his disciples. I wonder if the disciples aren't getting a huge kick out of his going after the pagans. But it's clear that while they were basking in his focus on the crowd, they had the same problem as the guy preoccupied with his inheritance. That ought to give us pause. These were some of the most fully devoted followers this world has ever known. Though they were committed followers, true-blue Jesus Nationals, they had missed the memo on becoming rich toward God.

What is important here is that the disciples didn't have a lot of money. They gave up that possibility when they gave up everything to follow Jesus. So for all of us who are skipping over these paragraphs because we don't have enough money to worry about overspending, slow down and consider the possibility that you can still be distracted from the pursuit of Jesus by the gravity of the material world.

Jesus turned to his disciples and said this:

Therefore I tell you, do not be anxious about your life, what you will eat, nor about your body, what you will put on. For life is more than food, and the body more than clothing. Consider the ravens: they neither sow nor reap, they have neither storehouse nor barn, and yet God feeds them. Of how much more value are you than the birds! . . . Consider the lilies, how they grow: they neither toil nor spin, yet I tell you, even Solomon in all his glory was not arrayed like one of these. But if God so clothes the grass, which is alive in the field today, and tomorrow is thrown into the oven, how much more will he clothe you, O you of little faith! (Luke 12:22-24, 27-28)

Jesus is after the fundamental fear that blocks our capacity to become rich toward God. It is the fear of not having enough, which inevitably leads to a disabling preoccupation with providing for ourselves. The antidote for being preoccupied with fear about provision is to believe, as Jesus says, that though "all the nations of the world seek after these things, . . . your Father knows that you need them" (Luke 12:30) and he will provide (see Luke 12:31). And a confidence in his willingness to provide will free us of the grip of fear, so that we will be able to live first and foremost to generously advance the Kingdom regardless of our wealth or lack thereof. Which, as he says, is how we become rich toward God.

GOD WILL TAKE CARE OF OUR NEEDS

Get the sequence here. When anxiety about material needs distracts you from your pursuit of national interests, it's a clear sign that you have stopped trusting God to provide for you. The national economy has a guaranteed plan. You give yourself to the things that matter most in terms of the nation, and the God who knows your needs will take care of you! Give yourself to the needs of people. Care about the lost. Be concerned about the poor and the oppressed. Give to the needs of those who can't help themselves.

It's about realizing that we can't take our money and material treasures with us . . . but we can send them on ahead. That is, in the Jesus Nation, our true wealth is measured by our investment not in material things but in what counts for God. But the tipping point is the point at which we can trust God to provide.

I was on my way to a Chicago Bulls game this past winter with a friend of mine. I should tell you that, unlike most of us, my friend feels no financial pain. And by that I mean that *he feels no financial pain.* In the course of our conversation, he told me that his daughter was getting married the next summer and that his future son-in-law had called him in September to ask for her hand. The conversation went like this:

My friend said to his future son-in-law, "What are you studying in school?"

The young man replied, "I'm working on my PhD in philosophy."

So my friend said to him, "How do you expect to support my daughter with a degree in philosophy?"

"I don't know," was the reply. "But we believe that God will provide."

"Do you plan on having kids?"

"We hope so."

"Well, how do you expect to support our grandkids with a degree in philosophy?"

"I don't know, but we really believe God will provide."

My friend pursued, "Do you think you'll buy a house?"

"Hopefully!"

"Then how will you make the house payments?"

The reply was the same: "I don't know. But we really believe that God will provide."

When he got off the phone, his wife said, "Hey, how'd that go?" He said, "I have bad news and good news. The bad news is this kid doesn't have a clue as to how he's going to support our daughter. The good news is he thinks I'm God."

When you feel you're getting sucked into Material World at the expense of the national interests of Jesus, remember that his national economy has a guarantee to those who follow Jesus into the needs of the hurting and the interests of eternity.

God will provide!

Stop being afraid, "for it is your Father's good pleasure to give you the kingdom." That is what frees you to "sell your possessions, and give to the needy. Provide yourself with moneybags that do not grow old, with a treasure in the heavens that does not fail, where no thief approaches and no moth destroys. For where your treasure is, there will your heart be also" (Luke 12:32-34).

And just in case you are thinking, *Why is it that God always wants my money?* He doesn't want your money; he wants your heart. And he knows that where you park your treasure, your heart will follow. You and I can come to church and tell Jesus he has our hearts. But he may very well respond, "Thanks for the words, but I'll know that by what you do with your treasure."

WHERE IS YOUR TREASURE?

I can tell a lot about you by watching you read your newspaper. If you are into current events, you'll go to the front section first. If your heart is into sports, you will turn to that section. If you are worried about your financial portfolio, it's the business section. If you are depressed, you'll look at the obits to see if you made it through the night. I don't need to ask; I just need to watch to know where your heart is. Jesus is saying that he knows where our hearts really are by watching what we do with our money.

I'll never forget the impact of reading a novel one January as Martie and I were basking poolside in the warm sunshine at a seaside resort. I was reading John Grisham's *The Street Lawyer.* The story opens with a lawyer dressed in his pin-striped suit and carrying his alligator briefcase, getting on the elevator to go to his office suite. As he punches the button for his floor, he notices an unkempt homeless man standing in the back corner of the elevator. As the attorney gets off on the sixth floor, he notices with surprise that the homeless man follows him. Stepping toward the receptionist, the homeless man opens up his coat and shows the receptionist the dynamite that's belted to his chest, demanding that all the partners of the firm gather in the boardroom. If they don't comply, he assures her that he will pull the string.

When the partners arrive, he lines them up along the walnut-paneled wall, shows them the dynamite, and proceeds to ask each one to tell him how much they made last year. After each of them responds, he then asks them how much they gave to the poor and needy. They all stammer to come up with a figure.

Then he asks the man in the pin-striped suit who prepares his income tax returns. When he learns that the returns are done in the accounting department, he has them faxed over. When the tax documents arrive, he asks the lawyer to read out loud how much each person in the boardroom earned in the last year, and how much each gave to the poor. Compared to the first number, the second was an embarrassingly paltry sum.

As I was reading, it was as if Jesus had showed up by my side and asked me, "How much did you make last year? How much did you give to what I care about? to causes that advance the Kingdom of God? to causes that make a difference in eternity? How much did you give to the needy and the poor?" Of course, without asking for my tax return he knew the answer to the penny. I don't think I will ever forget the impact of that moment on my heart and on my desire to really live to become rich toward God.

The economy of the Jesus Nation runs on the fuel of trust in the power of God to provide for our needs, which frees us to be generous both to those in need and to the cause of eternity. And that, by the way, is a great alternative to being tangled in the web of the greed and covetousness that drives us to be consumed with the nonstop obsession of getting all we want and more—yet at the end of it all, having nothing.

Buying into the national economy means turning our backs on greed and covetousness for the joy of generosity and contentment.

Chapter 20

WHO'S THAT KNOCKING?

AS I WRITE THIS, our economy is spinning into the vortex of a major global economic meltdown. Experts are telling us that it's the worst economic crisis since the Great Depression. Retirement plans are in the dumper. Home foreclosures are at record highs. Banks and other longstanding financial institutions that have been the bedrock of our financial system are closing or being bought or bailed out by our government. The crisis was the tipping point in a presidential campaign, and literally hundreds of thousands have lost their jobs.

According to the pundits, this disaster is due to the unrestrained greed that has run rampant for the last few decades. And there is plenty of blame to go around: Banks and financial institutions have made credit easy and actually encouraged skyrocketing personal debt; the government has deregulated the financial industry on the assumption that it can regulate itself; and we have leveraged the easy money and low-interest credit terms to help satisfy all our wants. Second mortgages were offered and taken so that we could buy that boat, that car, that second home, or whatever big-ticket item our hearts desired. And mortgage companies offered a long menu of enticing subprime loans so that we could buy the dream house with little thought of building equity. All this, in effect, left countless people financially upside down when their home values imploded, making them vulnerable to foreclosure and a pile of debt that would haunt them for years.

It reminds me of the ancient fable of the dog who had a juicy steak firmly gripped in his mouth. Crossing a bridge over a calm pond, he looked down and saw his reflection. Thinking it was another dog with what looked to be a larger steak, he opened his mouth to grab the larger steak—as his steak splashed into the pond.

THE DECEIT OF RICHES

Don't forget the warning label on life that we've already talked about: Take heed and beware of greed. Paul gives us three specific warnings when he writes about the great mistake of trusting in the uncertainty of riches. He says, "As for the rich in this present age, charge them not to be haughty, nor to set their hopes on the uncertainty of riches, but on God, who richly provides us with everything to enjoy" (1 Timothy 6:17).

First, wealth has a way of making us proud—or, as Paul puts it, haughty. Proud of our capacity to gain, of our houses, of our cars, of our clothes, of our accomplishments, of our vacations, of our very selves. And since we know that God resists the proud but gives grace to the humble (see Proverbs 3:34), we should humbly recognize that all we have is from him. As the text reminds us, he richly provides us with all good things to enjoy. Without his generously blessing us with the capacity to have wealth, we would have nothing. He is the generous provider, as we learned earlier. We are to be the grateful and humble recipients.

Second, it is easy to make the mistake of putting our confidence in—setting our hopes on—our wealth. I have several financial sites bookmarked on my computer: a page that keeps track of the few stocks that I own, another couple of pages that take me to the sites of my 401(k) plan, and the home page of my bank, where I can readily access the balances of my savings and checking accounts. I used to enjoy going to those pages periodically and watching the growth of my funds. My first instinct was to feel that I had plenty of resources and enough in my 401(k) to make it from retirement to heaven. But, with the advent of this global financial collapse, I have become very much aware that so much of it is smoke and mirrors. Watching my 401(k) plans morph into "201(k)" plans and my stock page disintegrate almost overnight has caught my attention and underscored again how vaporous our security is if we place it in our accumulated wealth. Paul gets it right when he reminds us about the uncertainty of riches.

But third, the most important aspect of the text is his call for us to trust not in the uncertainty of riches but in God. The subtle yet significant point Paul is making is that trusting in wealth puts trusting in God in tension. Or, to put it another way, if you have all you need, you will easily forget how desperately you need God.

THE SIN OF SELF-SUFFICIENCY

Jesus taught that we could not serve two masters, that serving money and serving Jesus are mutually exclusive. Paul puts a slightly different slant on the same thought. Of all the serious dangers of wealth, the worst is when we have enough that we feel like we don't need God. It diminishes the sense of our dependence on him. We have enough to fill our refrigerators, and we no longer need to pray, "Give us this day our daily bread." And when that happens, we are in a bad place. We are, in Jesus' perspective, though financially well off, actually impoverished.

Let me illustrate by telling you about people who lived in Laodicea, an ancient town in what we now know as Turkey. Laodicea was smack in the middle of major trade routes. The inhabitants were known for their expensive cloth from which the best clothing was made. They also had an exclusive on a salve that was in demand as a medicinal treatment for eye infections and disorders. All of this meant that they traded these commodities on the world market as traders passed through their town to buy the unique and high-in-demand products. They were flush with gold as a result and were known as a highly affluent community.

That was the good news.

The bad news was that their water was horrible, to put it mildly. Laodicea was built over water wells that were highly mineralized. The calcium and sulphur content made the water unbearable to drink. And, as though that was not enough, the water was tepid and lukewarm, which only accentuated the distasteful experience of taking a gulp from the Laodicean Waterworks. Though that was really bad news, the good news was that they were wealthy enough to build huge aqueducts that brought water from neighboring communities. To the north was a town known for its cold, clear, good-tasting water. The Laodiceans transported the cold, clear water from the north to their taps. To the south was a town with clear hot springs, and they moved that town's water through viaducts to their own town.

So, all was well in Laodicea. At least, from their point of view. They went to church on the weekends and then traded through the week and made more money. They bought all that they wanted to buy and financed all their needs with their deep pockets. How lucky that they lived in Laodicea! They had everything they needed.

But what they thought was good news was bad news, from Jesus' point of view. If you have grown up in the church, you know the story. In Revelation 3, we get to "eavesdrop" on a letter that Jesus directed the apostle John to write to the Christians in Laodicea. It is by far the most strident reproof of his letters to the seven churches. I find that interesting, because he writes to other churches about such problems as permitting heresy and false teaching in their churches or welcoming the Nicolaitans, a sect that believed in open and unrestrained sexual experiences in light of God's creation of our sexuality. In most of these church letters there is commendation for the good things the churches were doing, as well as a calling to attention the things that were displeasing to Christ. So, the fact that this is by far the most in-your-face reproof—and that it includes no word of commendation—makes me wonder, *What did they do wrong?* To say the least, it has my attention.

In the beginning of the letter, Jesus (through John) notes that they remind him of their water. "I know your works: you are neither cold nor hot. Would that you were either cold or hot! So, because you are lukewarm, and neither hot nor cold . . ." (Revelation 3:15-16). At this point, I can't help but reflect on how many times I have heard well-intentioned messages from this text about how we are lukewarm and need to fire up and get revival going again. "Be on fire for God; he doesn't like lukewarm Christians!" is the essence of the appeal. Well, it's true that Jesus is not pleased with lukewarmness, but it's not about catching fire for Jesus. If it were, he wouldn't have said that he wished they were either hot *or cold.* The lukewarmness that had Jesus so concerned was a far deeper problem. In fact, it was so serious to him that in essence he tells the Laodiceans, "You make me sick!" That's something I never want to hear Jesus say to me. He continues, "Because you are lukewarm, and neither hot nor cold, I will spit you out of my mouth" (verse 16)—most likely a polite way to speak about throwing up. This might seem a little over the top to us. But the Laodiceans understood. It's how they felt about their water.

He then explains what it is that is so disturbing to him about their lives: "For you say, I am rich, I have prospered, and I need nothing" (Revelation 3:17). We understand by inference, and in light of the letter's closing Jesus-at-the-door metaphor, that because of their affluence, they no longer felt like they needed Jesus. The old song I used to sing in church—*I need thee, O I need thee; Every hour I need thee! O, bless me now, my Savior, I come to thee*—was not in their hymnal.

If you have to give this problem a label, it is the sin of self-sufficiency. Their affluence had displaced their reliance on Christ, and though no doubt they went to church and probably did a lot of the right things, including giving to church programs, Jesus as a primary source and resource for their lives was not on their radar screens. If Martie were polite to me and did all the right things in our marriage, but because of her self-sufficiency never leaned on me for advice, input, fellowship, or companionship, I would take it personally and feel that something really big was missing from our relationship. I'd really be distraught if she had found someone else to be the source for her needs and looked to him for the advice, input, fellowship, and companionship that I desired to give her.

If I'd be distraught, I can understand how Jesus feels when we find a substitute for him and have our lives fully resourced, shutting him out of the place he deserves and desires. When we don't feel we need him, our prayers are perfunctory and rote. Our desire to go to his Word for direction, comfort, and assurance becomes nonexistent, leaving Bible reading to be a habit at best. We live lives that are conformed to his expectations but not connected to his heart.

THE AFFLUENCE AFFAIR

In Jesus' mind, affluence has the power to be an affair in the making. And, as Paul reminded us, it's an uncertain affair, at that. Throwing ourselves into the arms of its fickle flattery is not only an affront to Jesus, our champion and true lover, but is foolish since one day you may wake up and find it's all gone. Then what? And what if by God's astounding grace you can hang on to it? What do you do when you are old and its seductive joys are no longer interesting to you? What of the emptiness of your life then?

I find it interesting that Jesus Nationals in third-world countries where there is little in terms of affluence and wealth most often have a far more vibrant brand of followership than we do in the West. In China, Jesus Nationals have had a vibrant and contagious brand of Christianity. Chinese believers have been persecuted and in many cases excluded from the privileges of education and commerce; they have been relegated to the peasant class. Yet their walk with Jesus and their undaunted commitment to him has led to one of the most explosive cases of church growth in the history of the church. But China is changing. Global commerce has brought affluence and opportunity for wealth and personal advancement. Peasants are flocking to the major cities to secure jobs. Persecution is not as prevalent as it once was. And though this is good news in terms of social justice, my friends who work with the church in China tell me that it is taking its toll on the freshness, zeal, and commitment to Jesus that once marked the church in China. There is something about needing Jesus that takes us deeper and satisfies our longings more profoundly.

It's not that Jesus is upset that we have shut him out. This is not about a pity party in heaven. He's not feeling sorry for himself. In fact, he's feeling sorry for us. Jesus knows that when we substitute wealth for him, we have in reality become poor; and that wealth has not only deceived us but blinded us to our impoverished condition. He loves us and wants the best for us, which is why he says, "You say, I am rich, I have prospered, and I need nothing, not realizing that you are wretched, pitiable, poor, blind, and naked" (Revelation 3:17).

So, Jesus offers to enrich their lives with commodities that only he can provide. Commodities that will make them truly rich. He says, "Buy from me gold refined by fire" (verse 18), which is a reference to character. To people who work a lot just to get more cash, Jesus says what they really need is more character. To Jesus, who you are is far more important that what you have. At the end of the day, those people really need Jesus, because the wealth of good character is only found in him. Then he offers "white garments so that you may clothe yourself" (verse 18). The white garments refer to righteousness of life. Only he can model and provide true righteousness. Only Jesus can make you right deep down inside!

Once Jesus has offered to give them what they need to escape their poverty and nakedness, he offers them a remedy for their blindness: "salve to anoint your eyes, so that you may see" (verse 18). They have been blinded by their wealth to their real need for Jesus. So he offers them salve that will heal their eyes. This salve is the wisdom that only Jesus can give. It is the gift of seeing all of life from God's point of view. And that is exactly their problem. They have been looking at life from their own point of view, and it has left their lives and perspectives twisted, so twisted that they don't even think they need Jesus anymore.

It's fascinating to me that Jesus takes the three symbols of their self-sufficiency and reinterprets them in terms of the crying needs of their hearts. Jesus is saying to them, "You don't really have all that you need. What you really need is what you don't have, and that's a reliance on me to make you truly wealthy in terms of character, righteousness, and wisdom." No wonder he calls them to repent and to turn their hearts back toward him!

He ends the letter standing outside their hearts' doors, knocking, wanting to come in and fellowship with them so that they can find true satisfaction (see Revelation 3:20). Listen for the knock at your heart's door! He's got all you could ever want or need.

My friend Victor is a major leader in the church in Belarus. While visiting him several years ago, we traveled out into the country to visit his mom. We drove off the main highway for several miles and then turned right onto a rutted, two-wheel lane, until we reached a clearing in which was a little shanty village. We pulled up to Victor's mom's place. As she came running out, she was beaming. She hugged Victor for a long time, expressing her joy in repeated Russian phrases. And then, after we were all introduced, she led us into her little place. She had a garden, an out-house, and a pig in a pen.

I asked Victor about the pig, and he said she raises a pig in the summer and eats it in the winter. Inside there were only two rooms. We all huddled around her little table in the kitchen, and the joy never stopped emanating from her countenance. I thought she was just overjoyed to see Victor again. And she obviously was happy to see her son, but all of her conversation was about Jesus, how much she loved him and how much she was looking forward to seeing him in heaven. By the end of the afternoon, I had gotten a great lesson about what really counts in life. Jesus! This woman had nothing to speak of but had everything to speak about when it came to her satisfaction in him.

Chapter 21

MARVELOUS GRACE

NOTHING MARKS A PERSON as a devoted follower of Jesus more readily than active and generous grace being distributed from his or her life. It's a leading trait of Jesus Nationals. Before your eyes glaze over, let me remind you that John, after three years of intimate exposure to our national hero, our champion, was struck with the fact that Jesus' life was marked by the "fullness of grace and truth." And that the demonstration of this lead characteristic of his life was proof that he was who he said he was: "the only begotten of the Father" (John 1:14, KJV). And if the grace-truth combination was what Jesus was known for, then it needs to be the hallmark of our reputations, as well.

But, if my observations are true, for the most part we are pretty grace-less. We are way long on mad and short on mercy, particularly when it comes to politics and social issues. We are long on consternation and short on compassion when it comes to the hurting, the needy, and the oppressed. We tend to be pretty intolerant when others impinge on our space, our rights, or our privileges. We want others to give us space with our imperfections, but we rarely return the favor.

So, who needs to ratchet up the grace quotient?

• If you have been living with the expectation that everyone should be nice to you and you're put out when people don't shower you with the grace you think you deserve, then this chapter could be just what you need.

- If you think that acts of grace are weak and that being tough, intimidating, and manipulating is the way to make your world go around, you need to keep reading.
- If you think that grace is a nice theological thought unrelated to the rest of your life, it's important that you rethink that position.
- If you think that those around you really need a swift kick in the pants more than anything else, Jesus has a word for you.
- If you're stuck in the world of your past failures, if the offenses of others have robbed you of the joy of the present and the future, you desperately need to learn about the liberating power of grace.
- If you look at the homeless and say to yourself, "Why don't they get a job?" or you think that those who have contracted AIDS are getting what they deserve, then you desperately need this.
- If you tend to live on the grumpy, critical side of life; if your first instincts are to be judgmental; if you think that life is about keeping score, getting even, and making sure everything is fair, grace is probably a foreign concept to you.
- If you think that grace is the amazing thing that God has done for you with no thought of sharing it with others, read on.
- If you want to be like Jesus, an effective member of his nation, then it's time for you to embrace grace as the proof of your national identity.

When John wrote about Jesus in the prologue to his Gospel, you would think that he had an assignment to describe Jesus in twenty-five words or less. Well, actually it's twenty-nine, which only shows that it's hard to pin Jesus down to a word count. So here is John's conclusion about Jesus after three years of being up close and personal with him: "The Word was made flesh, and dwelt among us, (and we beheld his glory, the glory as of the only begotten of the Father,) full of grace and truth" (John 1:14, KJV).

It's important to note that the sense of the Greek in John's summary of Jesus is not that he is "full" of grace and truth. Literally, the Greek word means that he is the *fullness* of grace and truth. He totally embodies the entire essence of grace and truth. If you go to the ocean, for instance, and dip your little red bucket into the salt water, your pail will be full of the ocean—but it is not the fullness of the ocean. If Jesus is the fullness of grace and truth, then he is the entire ocean of it. All of his existence, actions, attitudes, relationships, and reactions demonstrate the breadth and depth of grace and truth, and there is no grace nor truth outside him.

Then John goes on to say, "And from his fullness we have all received, grace upon grace" (John 1:16). Or, to put it differently, where would you be without his grace? If we all got what we deserved, we'd be in a bad place. At its core, grace is about giving someone what he or she doesn't deserve.

But the impediment to our living out this national trait is the challenge of trying to do grace and truth at the same time. Life often puts us in the bind of not knowing whether to be truthful or graceful. Let's say you don't like the shirt your friend's wearing, and he says, "Hey, how do you like my shirt?" To tell the truth, you might say that it's really ugly. But if you choose grace, then what do you say? Trying to speak truth and grace at the same time often puts us in tension. God never struggles with that tension. And he doesn't lie or pamper us with empty flattery, either. He is, wonderfully, the totality of grace *and* truth. In this text, given its reflection on the glory of God as seen in Jesus' full embodiment of grace and truth, there is no conflict. In fact, it is a concept that you and I can easily embrace intellectually and theologically, and at the same time actualize it in our actions and attitudes.

Let's unwrap it.

The word meaning "grace" comes from the Greek word *charis. Charis* has several different English words that can express its meaning. Words like *favor, kindness,* and *helping*—particularly helping the helpless. Concepts like forgiveness and compassion are all grace equivalents. And the concept of doing something for the undeserving underlies all of the elements of grace. Grace is a mainstay in the descriptions of God in the Old Testament. The Hebrew word *hesed* is the word that describes God's loyal covenant love to his people. It was his posture in all of his actions and reactions toward his people. Regardless. And in the New Testament, the equivalent Greek word to the Hebrew *hesed* is the word *charis.*

When grace is combined with truth in the context of being the reflection of God, it becomes clear that John is not talking about telling the truth. There is a particular combination of words in the Old Testament used more than any other to identify the nature and character of God. In the Hebrew, it's *hesed emet,* which is translated as "steadfast love and faithfulness." This is the most consistently used description of the fundamental character of God. All Jewish people would have known that steadfast love and faithfulness were the hallmarks of their God. For instance, when Jonah finally fessed up as to why he didn't want to go to Nineveh, he cited this aspect of God's character. He said, "I made haste to flee to Tarshish; for I knew that you are a gracious God and merciful, slow to anger and abounding in steadfast love" (Jonah 4:2).

Most significant in trying to understand this grace-truth tension is that John refers to the grace and truth of Jesus as a reflection of the glory of God. In other words, it's a reflection of the *hesed emet* of God. If this is the case, then the truth that John refers to is not truth as the opposite of falsehood but as faithfulness and reliability. New Testament scholars such as Leon Morris and C. K. Barrett propose that John is referring back to one of the crucial moments in the history of Israel, at which God reveals his glory to Moses in the context of the golden calf story (see Exodus 32–34).[1]

Let's recall the scene. Moses has gone up onto the mountain with God, where he has received the Ten Commandments. Upon his descent, Moses hears the pagan music he heard in Egypt and sees the idolatrous orgy that is being played out at the foot of the mountain. He throws the tablets to the ground, goes back up the mountain, and asks God to show him God's ways in a time like this. In essence, he is asking God, "What are you like when people violate you like this? I know your ways when the Egyptians are coming after us. I saw you part the Red Sea. But what are you like now?" And then Moses said, "Show me your glory" (Exodus 33:18). And God said, "All right. I will. You won't be able to see my face, or you'll die. So I'll hide you in the cleft of the rock, and I'll pass before you and show you my glory." In the face of a phenomenal offense, God is about to reveal what kind of a God he is:

> The LORD descended in the cloud and stood with him there, and proclaimed the name of the LORD. The LORD passed before him and proclaimed, "The LORD, the LORD, a God merciful and gracious, slow to anger, and abounding in steadfast love and faithfulness, keeping steadfast love for thousands, forgiving iniquity and transgression and sin." (Exodus 34:5-7)

When God reveals his glory, he says, "I am a God of steadfast love and faithfulness." It's the *hesed emet* combination again. And I find this parallel far too compelling to draw any conclusion other than John's: "And we beheld his glory, the glory as of the only begotten of the Father, full of grace and truth" (John 1:14, KJV). John was looking back to everything he was taught in Sabbath school about God, and when he saw this combination worked out in the life of Jesus, he knew Jesus was the real deal. Jesus was indeed God as he claimed to be; he exemplified what John knew to be the central reality of God, that he was steadfast and faithful in his gracious love to his people.

Given the backdrop of what John is saying, *truth* in our text is not referring to propositional truth, as in 2 + 2 = 4. It's not referring to truth-telling, but truth-being, being true to who you are and what you claim to be. It is about being reliable and faithful. It's like saying, "The thing I like about you is that you are true to your word." That kind of true. "You're faithful; I can count on you." John is telling us that Jesus was the epitome of *reliable grace*. The issue then for us, if we are to live out this central characteristic of our nation's hero, if we are to be found in the way with him, is whether or not our lives are going to express to the undeserving people in our world the reliable grace that Jesus extended to us. This brings Jonah back to mind.

OBSTACLES TO GRACE

At the end of the day, Jonah's problem was that he refused to be the middleman in a grace transaction between God and a whole city of undeserving people. And, I might add, with good reason. Not a godly reason but, in fairness to Jonah, the kind of reason that our upside-down minds would quickly conjure up.

Nineveh was the enemy capital. It was violent, pagan, and bent on world conquest, which meant that Israel would be roadkill in any eventual advance of its army. And this army was not known for its kindness to its captives. In fact, ancient literature records that after conquering a territory, the Ninevites would decapitate the conquered populations and line the road back to Nineveh with pyramids of their heads. The generals were spared this particular fate but would be led back to the capital town only to be flayed like a deer, with their skins spread out on the city walls as trophies of the victory.

Jonah, determined not to be an instrument of God's grace, told a boatload of pagan sailors that, in essence, he would rather die than do grace on God's behalf. So they threw him overboard. But God was serious about his intentions, and he told a large fish to swim near the boat and pick up the reluctant prophet. Still determined not to do the work of grace, Jonah spent three days and nights in a sleazy underwater hotel before he finally said uncle!

Even then, when God showered Nineveh with his grace through Jonah, Jonah was unmoved (see Jonah 3:6–4:3). Seriously irritated with God for forgiving his enemies, he let God have it. Jonah reminds me a lot of the old Oreo ads. Nabisco tried to break all of us of the habit of pulling Oreos apart and eating the frosting in the middle, telling us, "Don't fiddle with the middle!" Jonah was forced into doing grace, but he refused to let God fiddle with his middle. On his own, he would despise Nineveh to the death, which God didn't let him do. Which made him really ticked at God.

God still calls Jesus Nationals to show off his lead characteristic by loving, forgiving, and blessing the undeserving. Do I hear you saying, "Yeah, but if you knew the people in my life, you'd know that they don't deserve it!" Thank you. That's just the point. If they deserved your love, forgiveness, kindness, and patience, it wouldn't be grace. Grace only works in the territory of undeserving lives.

So what would it mean for us to be people of reliable grace? Reliable grace is *the predictable action of abundant kindness regardless, even to the most undeserving offender.* It's the reality that as a part of the Jesus Nation, we live up to our identity by living in such a way that people can count on us to respond with grace.

Regardless.

It's unconditional. Even to the most undeserving of offenders. Here's a great Jesus Nation rule: *When in doubt, give grace!*

Right now, before you read another paragraph, put the book upside down and ask yourself who in your life could be a grace target, an opportunity for you to be a middle-person in a grace transaction between that person and your God. Is it your boss? Your spouse? Your friend? Your kids? That's your target. And, lest we forget, each of us is an undeserving offender in relation to God. Yet he reliably graced us with abundant kindness. It's time to pass it on! In a graceless, get-even, you-only-get-what-you-deserve world, grace from you to someone else will be proof positive that you belong to the Jesus Nation. It will make you different.

A true reflection of a holy nation because extending reliable grace is being different as God is different.

But before we can let grace prevail, we need to nuke the resistance points that tend to hold us back. So here are principles that will help you release the grace potential in your life:

1. Reliable grace is not a wink at sin; it's a solution to sin.
   Grace stops the food fights of life and interjects the power of love, forgiveness, and acceptance of the sinner. Solutions begin when grace shows up. Just look at the Cross. There is nothing quite as powerful as the words, *I love you regardless . . . I forgive you . . . How can I help you start the process of healing?*.

2. Reliable grace does not wait for repentance before offering forgiveness.
   Jesus Christ loved and forgave us two thousand years ago, and in love he urges us to come and tap the forgiveness that was made available at the Cross. Grace never waits for people to come groveling at our feet in humble repentance. Grace never lives in bitterness until someone repents. Reliable grace forgives regardless of whether someone asks for it or not. But when the offender comes, grace is already gift wrapped, packaged, ready to give. That's the way Jesus graced us two thousand years ago. Grace is not something we carry in a bag and give away when we feel compelled. It is who we are. It is a lifestyle. A character trait. Like Christ, we are to be the fullness of grace. Scratch true Jesus Nationals, and they bleed grace!

3. Reliable grace is not fair.
   For all of us bean counters who want to be sure that everything is always even and that the score remains tied, we need to know something about grace. Grace is not fair. And you can be really glad that God has not been "fair" with you!

4. Reliable grace doesn't make everything perfect.
   There will always be people who don't respond to grace. There will always be people who take advantage of our grace. The goal of grace is not to make everything perfect. It is to live up to our national identity and demonstrate that Jesus Nationals are people of amazing grace.

5. Reliable grace does not leave you vulnerable and weak.

    Acts of grace break the back of the destructive poisonous gas of getting revenge. I cannot emphasize this too much. Our grace to forgive somebody breaks the destructive cycle of bitterness and revenge. It sets the prisoner free. It gives us our future again. When in a grace moment you forgive someone, you are breaking the inevitable, despairing, destructive cycle of sin. That's what Christ did on the Cross, in the ultimate act of grace.

6. Reliable grace is not grumpy and critical.

    It is not complaining, but rather reaching out to be a part of the solution. Reliable grace faithfully tolerates others' weaknesses. I'm so glad that Jesus in his grace tolerates my weaknesses. I would be consumed in a moment if my hero and champion were not reliably gracious to be patient with me. Reliable grace gives us space to grow and develop and change.

7. Reliable grace leans toward the benefit of a doubt. It waits until all the facts are in.

    Jumping to graceless, judgmental conclusions can be an embarrassing experience, especially when the facts that finally emerge make you look silly and small. Some of us are slow learners on this one; we are forgetting that there are two sides to every story.

8. But most important, reliable grace forgives.

    Forgiveness may just be the flag that flies over the nation. There are few things that separate us more clearly from the fallen world around us than a willingness to forgive even the cruelest offense.

If the Jesus Nation's economy is driven by grateful generosity and trusting contentment, and if its national pastime is grace, then its national destination is glory.

Chapter 22

THE GLORY ROAD

I WILL NEVER FORGET the tragic day when the Bluffton University base-ball team was headed down to Florida to open their baseball season. As the bus driver was navigating his way through Atlanta, he misread the signs. He thought he was still on the interstate, but he was actually going full speed up the exit ramp, where the bus careened through the intersection, falling upside down back onto the main highway! The driver and his wife were killed, as well as five team members, and many of the other players were seriously injured. Certainly this terrible event reminds us, among other things, that it's important to know the difference between the road and the exit ramps.

It's that way with life, as well. It's easy to lose our way and easier still to think we are on the right way when in fact we are headed full speed for a serious collision. We need to constantly remind ourselves of God's warning in Proverbs 14:12: "There is a way that seems right to a man, but its end is the way to death."

If you are wondering what exit ramps and collisions have to do with God's glory, let me explain. First, God's glory is *the manifest radiance of all that he is in his all-surpassing, praiseworthy, stunning perfection.* His glory is his wow factor. When you see his all-surpassing, stunning, perfect love in action, all you can say is, "Wow!" It's the same when he manifests his mercy, power, righteousness, justice, grace, compassion, wrath, or any other aspect of his glory. And God, being invisible, has chosen avenues on which his glory would travel into visibility, so that it could be seen and experienced in real time and space.

One of his glory roads is creation. "The heavens declare the glory of God, and the sky above proclaims his handiwork" (Psalm 19:1). God's glory has traveled through all of history on the creation highway, and that road leads to every tribe, nation, and continent. From massive cities to the most remote corners of the earth, from the smallest flower happily surviving as it grows from a crack in a rock to massive rain forests with all their ecosystems, God's glory travels everywhere. Romans 1:19-20 reminds us that "what can be known about God is plain . . . because God has shown it. . . . For his invisible attributes, namely, his eternal power and divine nature, have been clearly perceived, ever since the creation of the world, in the things that have been made."

In other words, this communication of the creative, great, and sustaining work of God in all his awesome abilities is with us every day, from every new headline about discoveries in the amazing world of DNA and microbiology to the massive stretch of the universe on a clear night. The fact that we live in such an interesting world reveals that we have a wonderfully interesting God, who clearly is anything but dull and boring. Just think if the sky were colorless, if there were no clouds, no rain, no thunder and lightning, no wind to howl through the trees, and no breeze to cool us in the summer. Think of how dull life would be if food didn't taste good, if you had to eat merely the way your car needs to be filled with gas.

What if food had no color, if birds did not sing, if roses were not fragrant? If the vast stretches of the underwater world were not full of thousands of different species of fish, with such brilliant colorings that it must have drained God's palette a million times to get all their colors to be so perfectly stunning? Think of sunrises being without gorgeous colors, morphing from one to another for a half hour every morning. Think of what this world would be like if sunrises were as dull as turning on a flashlight, or if sunsets were only like turning off a light switch. I love seeing God's glory in the world he has created for our pleasure!

The nation of Israel was a chosen path on which God's glory would travel. God calls his people "Israel my glory" (Isaiah 46:13). God's amazing power would be made evident for all to see as they crossed the Red Sea on dry ground; his love and protection, as the Egyptian army was destroyed by the closing of the sea. So powerful was this testimony of the glory of God's power and protection that, according to the testimony of the local prostitute, Rahab, all of Jericho shook with fear as Joshua led his troops toward the walled city. His holiness would be glorified by the temple rituals; his grace and steadfast love, through his treatment of his often wayward and rebellious nation. A leading purpose in Israel's existence was to make the uniqueness of God's character and power rivetingly visible in a pagan world.

THE MAIN ROAD

Jesus was a glory road. As we saw in John 1:14, he was the express image of the glory of God in that we saw God's invisible qualities of reliable grace made manifest through his life. Later in that same Gospel, Jesus prays that God will glorify himself through him, acknowledging that already, "I glorified you on earth, having accomplished the work that you gave me to do" (John 17:4).

When God wanted to reveal his glory, he did it on the glory roads of creation, the nation Israel, Jesus, and—here's the incredible part—you and me.

When you were recruited for the Jesus Nation, you were put on the glory road with creation, Israel, and Jesus. Pretty classy company! As Jesus continued in his prayer, "The glory that you have given me I have given to them, that they may be one even as we are one" (John 17:22). He has given us his own glory, that we may be one. He has also charged us with bringing glory to him in all that we do: "Whether you eat or drink, or whatever you do, do all to the glory of God" (1 Corinthians 10:31). And "glorify God in your body" (1 Corinthians 6:20).

I was speaking at a banquet years ago where they had invited our whole family to attend. We were seated at the head table, the kind that is elevated at the front of the room, where all the big shots sit next to each other looking down on the commoners. After the meal, before the program had begun, my eight-year-old, Matthew, came behind the chairs and wanted to know if he could sit on my lap. So up he climbed. I need to insert here that I am an unrepentant people person, which means that when we would go out to a restaurant, I would often strike up a conversation with the server, calling her by name and inquiring about her day and anything else I could think to talk about with my newfound friend.

It usually drove our kids nuts. They would say, "Dad, just order. You're embarrassing us!" With that as background, you can understand my delight when Matt no sooner hit my lap than he read the name tag of the host of the evening sitting next to me, threw out his little hand, and said, "Hi, John. I'm Matt!" I loved it. He was a chip off the old block, and in that moment, he glorified his dad. Not much glory there, but the principle works. We are like chips off the divine block!

I have a friend who is an agent for professional athletes. He represents them by going to visit owners and managers of teams. He takes a large portfolio with pictures, stats, measurements, and anything else that he can get together to reveal to interested GMs the virtues of the players he represents. He's got a really cool job. He hangs with famous athletes, gets free tickets to the World Series and the Super Bowl, eats at the best restaurants, and flies first class. But none of that compares to the privilege we have as God's PR agents: Through our lives, the invisible God becomes visible, and a God who many think is unbelievable can become credible because they see him in us.

STAY ON THE ROAD

It's clear from God's Word that as citizens of the Jesus Nation, we are here for the purpose of living for the glory of God. In our journey on his glory road, it is our responsibility to move his glory forward in our world. And, in traveling through life to glorify God, getting lost is not a good thing. Among other things, let me give you three reasons why you can't afford to get off the road.

First, "you were bought with a price" (1 Corinthians 6:20). This is why, as we saw above, you must "glorify God in your body." God paid a great price to put you on the glory road. In this same passage, Paul reminds us that our bodies are the temple of the living God (see 1 Corinthians 6:19). There is an important connection here. In the Old Testament, God's glory resided in the Tabernacle in the wilderness and then in the Temple in Jerusalem. Today, we are the temple of God, his dwelling place, for the purpose of bringing glory to him. What a fabulous assignment and privilege!

Second, you can't afford to get lost because you would forfeit life's most profound privilege. To glorify God, to live on the glory road, is to make the invisible qualities of God visible in our world by living out his "transferable assets." For instance, when I commit a counterintuitive act of grace, I bring God's glory to my world. That's really precious cargo. There can be no greater privilege than being called to show off the dazzling realities of God. Where would you rather be traveling? On your little, dark, dingy, dead-end road toward self-glorification? Or would you like the privilege of delivering the glory of God to your world? I'll take the glory road!

Third, you can't afford to get lost because if you don't travel the glory road, how will your world—the world of your children, your work colleagues, your neighbors, your enemies, your fellow travelers—ever know what God is really like? There are many misconceptions about him that distort his reality and block others' interest in pursuing him. Don't feel any pressure here, but you may be the only one to help them change their minds about God.

If you need someone to keep you on the highway, fix your gaze on Jesus. MapQuest Jesus came to show us how to live out the glory of the Father. And to stay on track, think with me through three key questions.

Question 1: How do you know when you're on the glory road?

You'll know you are on the glory road when you are growing toward an increasingly greater expression of the glory of God by consistently and instinctively revealing the praiseworthy nature of God in every situation of life.

There are two key words here: *consistently* and *instinctively*. Consistency is important because there are a lot of tempting exit ramps from the glory road. Just this week Martie and I were wading through a situation with someone who had become an irritant in our lives in a pretty serious way. Have any people like that in your life? As is usually the case, we spent a lot of time reciting the horrible realities that had plagued us in our relationship with this person. And the more we rehearsed the list, the more frustrated and angry we became. And then Martie, in all of her spiritual maturity, said, "I don't think we are bringing glory to God in our attitudes about this person." My first thought was, *You're going to wreck all my fun.*

She went on, "The wonderful thing about God is that his love covers our sins, separates our sins from us as far as the east is from the west, and remembers them no more" (see Psalm 32:1; Psalm 103:12; Isaiah 43:25). She said, "Maybe it would be better if we figured out a way to love this person, pray for him, and seek God's wisdom on how we could find ways to be a part of the solution and not a part of the problem."

We made a choice right there to get back on the glory road. As life would have it, later that day I was chatting with a friend, and he began to talk about the concerns he had about this same person. It was an exit ramp off the glory road for me, and I had to decide if I would stay on the glory road and bring my friend with me or exit with him into the back alleys of talking behind our mutual friend's back. I chose to be consistent in my travels, so I said, "You know what we ought to do. God is a God of love and covers a multitude of sins, separating them from us as far as the east is from the west. Let's try to be God to him."

I had a choice. Bail on God's glory through me, or stay on the road and be consistent in my resolve to live to glorify God. Barricade the exit ramps! Consistency is the mark of someone who is maturing as a glory-road traveler.

As a consistent traveler, before you make a decision, you need to rock back on your heels and let your eyes glaze over and say to yourself, "What would God's glory look like in a moment like this?" Sometimes you'll have to search the Scriptures. Read the Gospels, and follow the actions and reactions of Jesus. But the consistent glory-road traveler doesn't do anything before being sure that it is consistent with the character and glory of God.

Over time, this process becomes more and more instinctive; because you've chosen to let his glory flow through you in similar situations, your heart will become trained and God's glory will become habitual. It's like driving to work. You've taken the curves and turns so many times that you really don't need to think much about it. It just happens, and you always get to the same place.

Be consistent, and it will soon become instinctive.

Question 2: What would God's glory look like on the road of your life?

What does God's glory look like? As we noticed in the previous chapter, Jesus is the expressed reflection of the glory of God: "The Word became flesh and dwelt among us, and we have seen his glory, glory as of the only Son from the Father, full of grace and truth" (John 1:14). John is telling us that Jesus came bearing the family resemblance. Hebrews 1:3

backs that up: "[Jesus] is the radiance of the glory of God and the exact imprint of his nature."

So keep your eyes on Jesus, and live out your commitment as a Jesus National to be found in the way with him. Watch his every move! He is God on our planet, pitching his tent among us, relating, interacting, responding. He never tarnished the profile of his Father throughout his life. He was consistent and instinctive! Watch Jesus manage relationships, watch him manage enemies, watch him manage sorrow and grief. Listen to him talk about money, hypocrites, power, prestige, trust, faith, and doubt. Read what the apostles wrote about him. Go to school on him. Philippians 2:1-11 would be a great place to start.

The more you know about Jesus, the more you watch him, the more closely you follow him, the more you can bring God's glory to your world. Early on in my pastoral ministry, I was walking into church one morning only to hear behind me a little boy ask, "Mom, is that Jesus?" I was all ears. She replied, "No, that's our pastor." What I wish she would have said is, "No, that's not Jesus, that's our pastor; but he reminds us a lot of Jesus." Had she said that, I would have known that I was on the glory road.

Just for starters, watch Jesus in John 9.

Seeing a blind beggar, the disciples stop and ask Jesus a question. No doubt this beggar had been the object of theological curiosity for a long time. My guess is that the scribes and the Pharisees had often spent time wondering why he was born blind. So, believing that Jesus always had the last word about these kinds of things, the disciples asked, "Why was this man born blind? Did his mother sin, or is it possible that the man sinned in his mother's womb?" (see John 9:2). To them, the beggar was no more than an object of curiosity. This is not unlike our tendency to want to know all the details about someone else's problem and then to second-guess why it is that they fell into the pit they are in.

Jesus was not merely curious. He had capacity to help, and this capacity would bring glory to his Father, who uses his power consistently to help the helpless and to lift up the fallen. So Jesus answered them that the man was born blind so that God could be glorified through his blindness. Jesus used his power to heal the blind man. And in that act of compassion, we see what God is like. God is not merely curious about our problems or theologically distracted. His compassion drives him to help and heal. You know you are on the glory road when you resist the exit ramp of curiosity and stay on the main road of compassion that consistently seeks to help and to heal, as God helps and heals.

I have a friend who went to a church to be on their pastoral staff. He had admired the senior pastor for years, and he couldn't wait to serve with him. In talking with him a few months after his move to the church, I asked him what it was like to work with this famous minister. He said, "It's great." He went on to volunteer what he was impressed with. He said, "The thing that is so remarkable to me is that when we're in staff meetings and a problem comes up, our senior pastor always says, 'What can we do to help?'" That was a glory moment. It may not seem remarkable to you, but if you have been around Church World for a while, you can identify with the reality that too often problems are encountered with a pointed finger and a grumpy response.

And here's an important clue. As we now know, our main identity in the Jesus Nation is that we are followers of Jesus. Not butchers, bakers, and candlestick makers. Sure, we have our occupations, but those occupations do not define us. We do our careers as followers of Jesus. We are not first and foremost Baptists, Methodists, Presbyterians, or Episcopalians. We do church as followers of Jesus. Consistently following Jesus is the key to knowing what God's glory looks like through our lives.

Often, Martie and I need to go somewhere in two cars. So, we agree to follow each other to our destination. It can be a frustrating experience if we don't keep our eyes on each other. Traffic gets in the way. I go too fast, or she goes too slow. You probably know how frustrating a caravan can be. But here is the good news: Jesus tells us to follow him, and he is always in clear view. He never takes an exit ramp. He is always headed straight for the glory of God. Even when the fog of life gets a little thick, watch Jesus' taillights!

Question 3: What does the glory-road traveler look like?

Since Jesus has recruited you as a national to travel on the glory road, what's the profile? John 1:14 gives it to us. Each phrase in the verse gives us an aspect of Jesus' life on the glory road.

First, the life of a glory traveler looks *incarnational*. The first thing we learn is that John portrays Jesus in terms of "the Word became flesh." It's important to note that John calls Jesus "the Word." Why doesn't he just call him Jesus? John is borrowing the concept from Greek philosophy.

Greek philosophers knew that out there somewhere in the universe was an unknown entity where all the issues of life were resolved, where all the questions of life were answered, where every mystery of existence finally took on meaning and purpose. Out there somewhere was the ultimate person, the ultimate place where all life finally made sense. They didn't know what to call it, so they called it *logos*, "the Word."

John, in his use of *Word* to describe Jesus, is making a shattering declaration. Jesus *is* the *logos*. The ultimate resolution to every question about life, the ultimate point of meaning and purpose is found and expressed in Jesus. What philosophers have longed for is satisfied in Jesus. But even more shocking is the statement by John that this *logos* is not an ethereal entity removed from our experience. He goes on to say, "This *logos* became flesh." Theologians call this the incarnation of Christ. The word *incarnation* literally means "in the flesh." Jesus became visible by inhabiting a body like ours.

I don't have the capacity to wrap my mind around, or find words that are fitting to express, the fact that the *logos* of the universe, God himself, decided to incarcerate his omnipresent spirit into the claustrophobic confines of a human body. Think of the *logos* being cradled in a mother's arms. Think of the *logos* experiencing sorrow and grief, of the *logos* being hailed one minute as a king and then crucified as a criminal. It is safe to say that the arrival of Jesus on our planet is unrivaled in human history. With the exception of the Resurrection, there has never been an event that is more profound or significant.

But it is more than a theological marvel. According to John 13–17, Jesus promised to send the Holy Spirit to dwell within us, so that after he left, we could pick up the privilege of showing off the reality of God through our lives. Which is exactly why Jesus prayed, "The glory that you have given me I have given to them" (John 17:22). That's a life-transforming truth. The Holy Spirit dwells in us, so that the glory God gave to Jesus can now be transferred to us by the Spirit's work. It's no wonder that Paul wrote to the Corinthians, "Do you not know that your body is a temple of the Holy Spirit within you, whom you have from God? You are not your own, for you were bought with a price. So glorify God in your body" (1 Corinthians 6:19-20).

We, too, are incarnational. We are clearly not Jesus, and we are not God. But Jesus dwells in our bodies in the person of the Holy Spirit for the purpose of glorifying God through our bodies. This is why Paul can say that you have "Christ in you, the hope of glory" (Colossians 1:27).

And it's why he underscores this profound privilege by writing that the mark of our spiritual maturity is that we are moving in degrees from glory to glory (see 2 Corinthians 3:18).

Incarnational living is the glory of God revealed through us, giving anyone who crosses our paths a personal, firsthand experience with the nature and the character of God. Incarnational living is God's glory with skin on it. Or, to make it more personal, it's God's glory with your skin on it.

The second aspect of a glory-road traveler's profile found in John 1:14 is that we are not only incarnational, but we are *locational*, as well. Notice that our text says that Jesus came and dwelled with us. Literally, he pitched his tent among us. Jesus had a lot of options. He could have come on location here and taken a penthouse condo in Jerusalem with security guys at the gate. He could have run with those who hung out in high places and fancy restaurants in Jerusalem, or displaced the high priest. But it's important to understand how dramatic his chosen placement was. When the glory of God visited our planet incarnationally in the person of Jesus, he pitched his tent among *us*.

Among common folk like fishermen, despised tax collectors, rich young rulers, prostitutes, Pharisees, and the blind, hungry, and hurting. He camped out with them all! He went where they worked, he went where they played, he went where they worshiped. The glory of God was among us—on location.

If you and I are following Jesus on the glory road, then we, too, have to be incarnational on location. There ought to be a sign on your desk that says, "GOD WORKS HERE." Well, it's probably best not to try that; but your boss ought to be saying, "You know, I have nobody quite like you in my office. You give me a good day's work, you are faithful to the task, you are a person of integrity, and I can trust you." It all about incarnation on location.

How about at home? When Ephesians 5:25 says, "Husbands, love your wives, as Christ loved the church," it sounds incarnational on location at home. Or, when we read a little further that fathers should not "provoke [their] children to anger, but bring them up in the discipline and instruction of the Lord" (Ephesians 6:4), that's incarnation on location! On location in the car, on the golf course, in your neighborhood. On location with your friends and also with your enemies. On location in your yard. We're stewards of God's creation. I figure my yard work is about reversing the Fall and restoring the beauty of God's creation. I don't think it glorifies God if you're the person in your neighborhood who reseeds everybody's yard with dandelions.

Staying on the glory road is about being incarnational on location. Wherever you are, wherever you go, you pitch your tent among the people there for the glory of God.

Which leads us to the third aspect of the profile in John 1:14. God's glory through us is *observable*. Notice that John says, "And we have seen his glory." People may not want to listen to what you have to say about your walk with Jesus or about his exclusive claims. But, guaranteed, they are watching you. From your children at home to the people in your office, you are being watched! The disciples watched Jesus for three intensive years, twenty-four hours a day, and they saw God's glory.

Fourth, God's glory through us is exactly that: God's. It is his glory that we are living for and not our own. Jesus could have lived for his own glory. He had all the pizzazz. But he kept reflecting the glory to his Father. Our text tells us that the incarnational, on location, observable glory of Jesus was the "glory as of the only Son from the Father." They saw the Father in him. This may be the trickiest part of staying on the glory road. As soon as you do something to make the glory incarnational, locational, and observable, people will notice and often applaud you for doing something good. And the exit ramp of pride and personal glory looms large and almost irresistible. If you are really patient with someone, inevitably someone will say, "I have been watching you" (observation on location); "you are a very patient person" (incarnational). If you aren't careful, the glory will turn to you and not to God.

It was a rather routine discussion that was taking place at the elders' meeting when I decided to get up and refill people's coffee cups. I have always been a fan of following Jesus as a servant. Leaders are first and foremost servants, so I thought I'd do the coffee drill. While I was pouring the coffee, one of the elders said, "Wow, our pastor is a servant leader!" I have to say that I liked hearing him say that. So at the next meeting, I couldn't wait to pour the coffee again. Only this time it was not motivated by showing Jesus' servant attitude through my life (as is exemplified in Matthew 20:20-28 and Philippians 2:1-11) but hearing someone pat me on the back again about what a great leader I was.

God takes it seriously when we steal his glory from him. As we have noted before, Nebuchadnezzar took the glory of God for himself, and

God turned him out into the field where he ate grass like a beast for seven years. When someone applauds your patient reaction to a stressful situation, it's instinctive to say, "Well, thank you. I do my best to be patient." But if that's your response, all I can say is that you must like grass!

Does it ever cross our glory-robbing minds to say, "Well, actually, I'm not a patient person, but God's been so patient with me that I'm trying to show his patience to others." Or, how spot-on would it have been for me to say to the elders, "Thanks, but Jesus showed me how to do this." Of course we have to be careful not to be corny or sanctimonious, but looking for ways to reflect the glory back to God is what Jesus Nationals do.

One of my all-time favorite sports moment was Bernhard Langer's Masters victory on Easter. He came up the eighteenth fairway at Augusta National Golf Club and sank the winning putt to the roar of the crowd. They put the green jacket on him and asked him in front of a national TV audience if this was the greatest day in his life. He replied, "This is the greatest day in my golfing career, but it doesn't compare to the fact that two thousand years ago today my Lord and Savior died and rose again to give me eternal life." Wow. I was off the couch in the excitement of the moment. God was glorified as Langer turned the spotlight from himself to his God

It's not our glory; it's his—pass it on.

And last, God's glory through us is *verifiable*. The glory that John saw was authentically just like the God he knew: the fullness of grace and truth. Jesus came and claimed to be God, and his disciples watched him and recognized God. The glory was verifiable and authentic. How do we show God's glory in a verifiable, authentic way?

Obedience and surrender are the key. Jesus continually talks about surrendering to the will and glory of his Father. So simple, isn't it? But that's exactly how it happens. If we want to glorify God in a verifiable and authentic way, we will obey him by surrendering to his will. He is the fullness of glory, so obedience to him guarantees that we are traveling on the glory road. He is a forgiving God, so when he commands us to forgive and we obey, we bring glory to him and resist the tempting exit ramps of bitterness and revenge. He is a generous God, so when we obey and give to the needs of others, we are expressing his glory. He is a righteous God, so when he calls us to righteousness and we obey, we bring glory to him. He is a serving, just, merciful, holy God, so when he commands us to activate qualities like that in our lives, his glory becomes verifiable and authentic.

Something really weird happened not long ago. I've been living in America for a long time, and I have never seen anything quite like this in my life. The prime minister of Japan visited America. Normally the president throws black-tie dinners at the White House and press conferences in the East Room when heads of state visit. But since the Japanese prime minister is an Elvis fan, his big desire was to go to Memphis to visit Elvis's home. Get this: President George W. Bush flew him on Air Force One to visit Graceland. And then the prime minister of Japan got up and serenaded President Bush with an Elvis song. How strange is that?

People tend to glorify their heroes by talking about them and acting like them. In fact, in the case of Elvis, many fans refused to believe that he had died. For years after he died, we heard about Elvis sightings. Nobody wanted the king to die.

Thankfully, our King is not dead. He is here, dwelling in you, for the purpose of giving your world Jesus sightings in incarnational, locational, observable, and verifiable ways. It is our profound privilege to live out our lives on the glory road.

My mind runs to that good old song by another legendary crooner, Willie Nelson:

> *On the road again*
> *Just can't wait to get on the road again . . .*
> *Goin' places that I've never been*
> *Seein' things that I may never see again*
> *And I can't wait to get on the road again.*

Here is a prayer for all of us who are ready to take the glory road as followers of Jesus:

> Lord, I surrender everything I am and have to your glory by intentionally seeking to use each opportunity of life to glorify you. Help me to provide others with a personal experience of your true nature and character, which dwells within me in the person of your Holy Spirit for the purpose of living your glory out through me.

Chapter 23

SWEET SURRENDER

HAVE YOU EVER NEEDED to get somewhere but couldn't get on the right road? Detour signs abounded, but in the confusion and traffic you missed the arrows and were lost? There is no need to feel that way about following Jesus on the glory road—unless, that is, you miss the signage! There is only one entrance ramp to the glory road, and it is marked "Surrender."

Under the large print on the signage is the phrase "Not I, but Christ!" In fact, if we're going to understand the key to consistency on the glory road, we need to live out the truth of Galatians 2:20: "I have been crucified with Christ. It is no longer I who live, but Christ who lives in me. And the life I now live in the flesh I live by faith in the Son of God, who loved me and gave himself for me."

In other words, "I die; Jesus drives."

We have missionary friends all over the world, so we get lots of prayer letters, with lots of fascinating stories. But the story that tops them all came from our friends Dale and Carmen, who work in Romania. Soon after moving in, they made friends with an elderly couple next door, praying that this couple could be the first ones they led to the Lord. One day, Carmen got a phone call from the old lady next door, who said, "I've got a problem. Two days ago, they took my husband to the hospital. And he died this morning. They want me to come and get him." Strange, but this is the custom in Romania. "But since I don't have a car, could Dale go and get him for me?"

Needless to say, Dale didn't know what to expect. Would the body be in a zipped-up bag, or what? But to his surprise, it was fully dressed, lying on a table. So he picked up the dead man and tried to fit him in his tiny missionary-size car. Unfortunately, the corpse didn't fit in the trunk or the backseat. So his only option was to set it upright in the front passenger seat, next to him. But the corpse kept falling over. So, he seatbelted it and drove the corpse home in the front seat next to him. As I read the story, I didn't know whether to laugh or cry. The thought of seeing Dale with the dead man strapped in next to him, head bobbing as they drove down the street, was almost too much.

But the picture is not too far removed from the one Paul gives us in Galatians 2:20. Jesus wants you strapped next to him, and he wants you to die to yourself and let him drive. Because the mystery and magic of the text tells us that though we have died, we are yet alive with him. The only difference is that in our new life on earth, after we have died to ourselves, he now lives through us, which obviously guarantees our staying on the glory road.

CRUCIFIED WITH CHRIST

This Galatians text details a two-step process to this "I've died and am alive" type of surrender to Jesus. Step one is to constantly verify a personal DOA (dead on arrival) report on yourself.

Keep the self crucified.

When Paul says, "I have been crucified with Christ," he uses the perfect tense. Understanding that it's in the perfect tense is very important. The perfect tense in Greek indicates a past reality with ongoing results and ramifications. For instance, let's just say that someone walked up to you and knocked you out with a punch and left you with a swollen eye and a bloody nose. That would be an act of history. But it is more than a historical fact. It is a fact about a past action that has ongoing implications. A black eye for several days and a call to your lawyer (not recommended) may be among the continuing results from the past action. Or, if you throw a rock into a still pond, there will be not only a splash marking the initial action, but also the ongoing results in the circling waves that wash toward the shore. This is what the perfect tense seeks to convey. What

Paul is driving at is that we have been crucified with Christ and that the past reality has important, ongoing implications in our lives.

So let's talk about the past reality. What happened when Jesus died? Well, a lot of things happened when he was crucified. But after the agony of that torture, it was a decisive death. Nobody ever wrote a book on five ways to survive a crucifixion. If you're crucified, you die.

The crucifixion of Christ was not only a denunciation of sin and hell and a demonstration of the agonizing outcomes and penalties of sin; it was also a decisive victory over sin, death, and hell. And, it was more than Jesus dying *for* you; Paul indicates that as his followers, we died with him. To make his point unavoidably clear, he attaches the Greek preposition for "with" to the word for crucifixion, so that it becomes one word. In English, it would be a brand-new word that would look like *withhimcrucified*. Paul wants us to see that there is no separation between Jesus dying for us and us dying with him. When you joined the Jesus Nation, you essentially came to the Cross, admitting that your sins were a deep offense to God, which left you hopelessly guilty before him. You pled for his forgiveness and mercy. At that point, in a very real sense, you and all the garbage and baggage of your past life *were crucified* with Christ. . . . You died!

That's the past reality. Now that past reality, according to Paul's framework, has present implications. To capture the meaning of the perfect tense, the King James translates it, "I am crucified with Christ." You continue to be a person who is crucified with him . . . every day . . . 24/7.

Clearly, we have a problem here, because we don't tend to live like that. Jesus decisively defeated all the garbage of the sin in your life when you died with him. Why is it then, that on the other side of the Cross, you go back and dip into the garbage pile again? We don't live like that in the material areas of our lives. When I ask Martie what we're having for supper tonight, she has never said, "Tonight we are having garbage. Why don't you go out to the garbage can in the garage and get some of those old banana peels, those old melon rinds, and some of those broken egg shells—oh, and bring in the bacon that we didn't eat three days ago." Never. And, unless we were destitute, none of us would ever think of living like that. We have died to our garbage, so why do we keep dredging it up?

I need to confess to you how difficult it is for me to stay dead to myself in heavy traffic. It's always been a frustration to me that as a follower of Jesus I don't have enough gestures to use in traffic. But I have had tons of out-of-body experiences when I end up watching myself resurrect attitudes and actions in traffic and then say, "Joe, was that you?" Well, that's exactly the problem. It was me, and not Christ!

One colossal resurrection of "me" happened in my first pastorate. It was a growing church plant, which meant that the pastor still did most of the grunt work. I remember walking into church one morning and having the Sunday school superintendent say to me, "Hey, Pastor, don't forget to order next quarter's Sunday school material." I said, "Okay, no problem." And I didn't procrastinate. I just totally forgot it.

The next Sunday when I walked in, the Sunday school superintendent said, "Hey, Pastor, did you order the Sunday school material?" To this day I can't believe how easily and quickly this resurrection occurred to save my pastoral reputation from damage. "Yes!" was my immediate response. I remember going into my office and opening my briefcase to get out my sermon notes. It was as though the Holy Spirit appeared on my desk and said, "So, you're the truth teller today? You just lied to the Sunday school superintendent, and you're going to tell people the truth of God's Word?" I knew what I had to do. I had to crucify the garbage that I had just resurrected and call the superintendent into my office to ask his forgiveness for lying to him. Tough assignment. Especially when the old me kept saying that I could call FedEx in the morning, and the guy would never know that I hadn't ordered it. But I knew I had to die again to myself, give myself an autopsy to make sure I was dead, and release Jesus to live through me.

We're like graveyard Christians. When we need a lie to get us out of trouble, we walk into the graveyard and do a resurrection. Dead man lying, come forth. When we need a little adrenaline rush, dead man lust, come forth. We call up dead man greed to satisfy our fleeting wants. Jesus didn't put to death all that stuff so that we could sneak back into the graveyard and stage our own little resurrection shows.

What Paul is saying here is that we need to give ourselves an autopsy that never stops. Every day, check to make sure the pulse of your sinful nature is flatlined.

The sooner you die to yourself, the happier your spouse will be, guaranteed; the happier your kids are going to be; the happier your work colleagues are going to be. When you die to yourself—in fact, when you stay dead and let Jesus live through you—your whole world is going to like it a lot better. More important, the sooner we die with Jesus, the sooner God's glory will begin to flow.

Which brings us to the second step of actualizing life on the glory road.

Live out the fullness of Christ.

Our text, Galatians 2:20, tells us that "Christ . . . lives in me. And the life I now live in the flesh I live by faith in the Son of God, who loved me and gave himself for me."

In order to live out the fullness of Christ, we will need to get a grip on three dynamics in this text that enable us to release the power and presence of Jesus in our own lives, as well as from our lives to the lives of others. The first dynamic is being willing to both recognize and release the new resident within us: Christ. When we were saved into his nation, the Holy Spirit entered us, and according to Jesus' upper-room discourse (see John 13–16), that resident is Jesus in the person of the Holy Spirit. As we've discussed, Jesus is the manifest glory of God, a chip off the divine block. As John says, though no one has seen God at any time, Jesus came to show us what God is like (John 1:18). And to top it all, Hebrews 1:3 exclaims that Jesus is "the radiance of the glory of God and the exact imprint of his nature."

This perfect, radiant reflection of the very nature of God lives in us for the purpose of demonstrating God's reality through us. Which is why you and I need to die. As we have noted before, we are born fallen with the imprint of everything that contradicts the nature of God tattooed to our emotions, thoughts, will, and desires. We need to die to ourselves so that he can emerge. It's just that simple. It's just that challenging.

In the early spring of 2009, Susan Boyle took the stage of the British version of *American Idol*. She was not much of a sensation to look at, compared to the contestants who had taken the stage before her. In fact, you might say that's an understatement. Obviously older than the usual contestants and wearing a rather common dress, she stood there all alone on the stage, in front of a skeptical audience that obviously thought her presence was some kind of a joke. Until, that is, she raised the mic to her mouth and began to sing.

Spellbound, the judges were clearly taken with the beauty and power of the voice that filled the auditorium. That once-skeptical audience was on their feet, cheering with delight. The video clip hit the YouTube circuit, and in just a few days literally millions of people had seen and heard a rivetingly attractive song from what seemed like an unlikely source.

All of us are unlikely sources when it comes to the beauty of Jesus flowing out of us. But that is how he planned it. Common folk like you and me were brought into his nation to take our turn on the stage of life in front of the skeptical audience of our world, so that anyone who crosses the path of our lives would see the unique beauty and glory of Jesus emerging from our lives. Asked why she entered the contest, Susan said that she had promised her mother that she would, just before her mother passed away. Susan kept her promise and blessed a beleaguered world. Make a promise today to the one who lives within you to let his compelling reality flow from your life, so that you can bless your world with his presence in the person of *you*.

We do this, Paul goes on to say, "by faith in the Son of God." The way you release the reality of Jesus out from your life, Paul says, is to consistently practice what I call *faith surrender*. As he says, "I live my life now in the flesh by faith in the Son of God" (see Galatians 2:20).

First of all, let's unwrap the word *faith*. Faith is believing in someone or something outside of ourselves that enables us to act according to the belief. Silas, my grandson, is at the age at which he likes to jump into my arms. It's easy to do it when I am six inches away, but as I get back farther he pauses and thinks it all through. It's a faith process in action. Will I be able to catch him if he jumps that far? Will his belief in me outweigh the chasm and danger that lurks between us? But after weighing all the factors, he jumps. And I catch him, and all is well. In fact, he wants to do it again. And the more he does it, the shorter the time it takes for him to jump. His faith grows by his experience.

We trigger the glory of God in our lives by faith. It's hard to jump across the chasm of forgiveness, of sacrificially giving our money away, of loving a spouse when we feel vulnerable. But faith in God's Word and the belief that obedience is in everybody's best interest enables us to proceed. And as we jump, the glory of God's forgiveness, sacrificial generosity, and unconditional love emerges from our lives. Faith is always a surrender. By faith we surrender to God's will that so often seems counterintuitive. We surrender our dreams when necessary because we believe by faith that his dreams are better for us. We surrender our comfort when necessary. We surrender our own self-interests. Faith is a surrender word. And when we surrender to his Word and will, we align ourselves with his nature and unlock our capacity to reflect his image in every situation of our lives.

If the word *surrender* bothers you, making you feel out of control and vulnerable, I wouldn't blame you. Except, that is, for the mutuality of surrender that we experience in Jesus. As Paul says, "The life I now live in the flesh I live by faith in the Son of God, who loved me and gave himself for me" (Galatians 2:20). This surrender is not spiritual robotics or even mere spiritual responsibility. It's reciprocal. We live to reciprocate his amazing love for us. You die to yourself to reciprocate his amazing death for you. In other words, you and I surrender to him because he surrendered to God for us. This is a relationship. He put his arms wide for you on the cross. He died for you, and because of that, you today have all that you have in him. When you say, "How can I thank you, Lord?" He says, "Die for me, so that I can live through you."

Every time I read the story of a martyr, I ask myself if I would ever be willing to die for Jesus. I think it's a big question. But as I was studying this text, I realized it's not a question about future what-ifs. I have an opportunity every day to die for Jesus. Every time a lie would get you out of trouble, you have an opportunity to die for Jesus. When revenge, gossip, selfishness, or a response lacking compassion feels really good— you have a chance to die for Jesus. And when you die for him, the glory starts to flow.

His death on the cross triggered the glory of God in bold dimensions. When Jesus died, we saw and experienced the love of God in all its encompassing breadth and depth. Dying on the cross, Jesus put the justice of God in full view. We saw his mercy in action and the holiness of God being satisfied. We saw that God is willing to serve us to meet our most fundamental needs and that he is a God of sacrifice when necessary to serve our deepest dilemma. The glory of God has never been so apparent in all its fullness as when Jesus died for us.

And we can't overlook the fact that Jesus' death was preceded by the agony of Gethsemane. Triggering the glory of the Cross required surrender in the garden. We must always keep in mind that agonizing moment when Jesus knelt at the rock, pleading, "Father, can we do this some other way?" (see Luke 22:42-44). There will be times in your life when faith surrender is really hard. And surrendering, dying to yourself, will be really hard. Kneel there with him. Share his agony until you say with him through lips parched with the strain, "Not my will, but thine be done" (verse 42, KJV).

Before Jesus died on the cross to show us God's glory, he had to die to himself.

Go to Gethsemane. Be at the rock with him. Of course, faith surrender is going to be challenging and the requirements of God daunting. But in the end you will never regret saying those sweet words of surrender, "Not my will but thine be done!"

Bonnie was a student at Moody when I was serving there. She was an energetic, vivacious, super college student. She babysat for our grandkids. She nannied for people who lived two floors above us. And every time we were on the elevator with these people, they'd say, "Wow, are all of your students at Moody like her? We love Bonnie. She's terrific." She fell in love with one of our guys from the UK, a "football" player named Gary. They got married and gave their lives to serve Jesus in Lebanon. They were well aware of the dangers of going to Lebanon but believed that God was leading them there. Bonnie went to work in a clinic for refugees' children to bring Jesus to those lost, lonely kids. Gary was a street evangelist.

One morning, Bonnie got up early to go open up the clinic. Gary, who had come in late from street work the night before, was still sleeping. She slipped out of the bedroom and went to start her day ministering to children. Soon after she had opened the clinic, there was a knock on the door. She opened it and found herself face-to-face with a hostile Muslim whose anti-Christian feelings had been incited at his mosque the day before. He lifted a gun and shot her in the face four times, point-blank. She died as a martyr that day.

A friend from the clinic called Gary, so upset that he spoke incoherently and could hardly get the news out. Gary, knowing something bad had happened, grabbed his clothes, jumped into a taxi, and headed for the clinic. As he ran from the taxi, someone shouted to him, "Gary, Bonnie has been shot. Bonnie is dead! Bonnie is dead!" As he ran frantically toward the door of the clinic he was stopped by the police. He pleaded with them, but they refused to let him in.

He fell to the ground and in that moment realized that he had a choice. He told me later that as he lifted his face, he could see Bonnie's legs through the door and the pool of her blood. As he pounded his fist on the ground, he prayed to God, knowing that he could hate the assassin and seek revenge, or choose immediately to forgive him and continue to try to reach the Lebanese for Jesus. He told me, "Joe, it was like the war went on for an hour. It wasn't that long, but it seemed eternal at the time."

And then he said, "I knew what I had to do. I would forgive them, and with agonized determination the words came out of my mouth: 'God, I choose to forgive them. I will forgive them.'" That faith surrender triggered the visible evidence of a loving and forgiving God through his life. The depth of his struggle and the piercing reality of his loss only made God's glory more evident. The tougher it is to die to ourselves, the greater the glory of God through our lives.

There's only one on-ramp to God's glory, and its sign says "Surrender." Welcome to life on the glory road, the main road through the Jesus Nation.

Chapter 24

JESUS IN JEANS

HE TOLD ME HIS NAME was Emmanuel! Just like that, he blurted it out. No sense of embarrassment. No sense of exaggerating his own worth. Just, "Emmanuel."

I tried not to look surprised as I said, "Excuse me, but what was your name again?" I was thinking that I could get away with a second stab at getting acquainted because he had told me his name in broken English. In reality, it was not that I couldn't make it past the accent. I had gotten the name right. But getting the name right was exactly my problem. Who on earth would be so bold as to give their child a name that, as I had always felt, was the exclusive property of Jesus? My mind was connecting the dots to the place in Scripture where the angel told Joseph about Mary's carrying Jesus. This was to fulfill a prophecy from Isaiah that the virgin would conceive a child called Emmanuel, which meant "God with us" (Matthew 1:20-23). And, if I remember correctly, that only happened once!

Searching for a way around the awkwardness, I said, "How interesting! Do you know what your name means?" To which he readily replied, with a sense of unusual confidence and pride, "Yes! God with us!" I actually thought, *You should blush when you say that!*

But he didn't.

He was shameless about his name.

The fact that his name meant "God with us" hardly seemed appropriate on that May morning in a crowded, dingy room in a Romanian seminary. At least, not if he was the living manifestation of the presence of Jesus in our midst. I had noticed him while I was speaking. It's amazing the kind of thoughts that go through your mind when you look at the people who are listening to you preach.

Actually, it would have been hard not to notice him. Three rows back on the aisle, slipped down in his chair, he was wearing a cap with some indistinguishable logo on it, an off-green T-shirt that paraded the brand name Diesel, and a pair of well-worn jeans. He had stood out to me because all the other young men were in white shirts and ties; the women were equally dressed up.

If indeed God had been with us, I would have expected something far more spectacular. More proper. Like showing up in a pinstripe suit to out-proper everyone else in the room.

I couldn't get that encounter with the seminary student out of my mind. And the more I thought about it, the more I sensed that far from being out of touch with reality, the student actually had it right. He was right about something that I might not have thought about for a long time. If ever. Like the fact that we are supposed to be "God with us" in our world. And that being "God with us" is not just another thing that we are supposed to be—we've all had enough lectures about all that we are supposed to be—but rather, the primary mark of what it means to be followers of Jesus, dedicated Jesus Nationals.

When was the last time that you thought of your life in terms of the all-consuming privilege of liberating God from the "friendly confines" of Church World and taking him to the streets? of becoming a "middleman" in a divine encounter between God and your world? of making the moments of your life strategic opportunities to take the lid off God's ways, words, attitudes, and perspectives and pouring a transforming dose of the divine into your relationships, your careers, and even casual encounters?

When we get a grip on the Emmanuel Factor—or should I say when it gets a grip on us—we wake up to this stunning reality: Becoming the presence of God in our world is a lot better than what we bring to the world on our own. And in case you think that you're sharp enough to "do" your world better than God would, ask your spouse, your friend, your boss. They will assure you that they prefer God through you rather than you all by yourself.

Still, I'm afraid that to a lot of us the thought of becoming the presence of God in our world probably feels a lot like typical church talk. A little beyond most of us. *I mean, after all, do I have to be the "consuming fire of his glory," with "a voice like many waters" and "a tongue like a mighty sword"? And walking on water, much less parting it, seems a little past my capacity even on a good day. And what would I wear? Robes decked with sapphires and rubies, a tall gold pointed hat and a bronze breastplate? That's not exactly my thought of trendy fashion.*

Which was sort of what I was thinking about the student three rows back in chapel in Bucharest, Romania. *Look, if you are "God with us," what are you doing in a Diesel T-shirt, a cap, and beat-up jeans?* I didn't notice the shoes, but it would have been cool if they had been sandals. Based on the way most of us think about Jesus, if you were to try to be him to your world, you might think that you should show up in something fitting to his position as the creator of the universe, something regal and splashy.

But here is a liberating thought. When Jesus arrived on our planet, claiming to be God, he didn't try to outdress the chief priests of his day who had getups worth staring at and really cool hats that made them stand out in a crowd. He dressed just like any other guy, just like you and I would dress if we had been alive then. I don't know about a Diesel T-shirt, but "he had no form or majesty that we should look at him, and no beauty that we should desire him," as the prophet Isaiah foresaw (Isaiah 53:2).

It was just plain Jesus in jeans! Jesus in jeans so that common folk like you and me could believe that we could walk in *the way* with him. Jesus in jeans so that we could watch him do life on his terms, in our world. Jesus in jeans so that we would know that we could take *the way* to others, so that they, too, could know what life in the Jesus Nation is really meant to be.

Jesus' coming as one of us commoners was the beginning of a lot of surprises. He was anything but what you might have expected him to be. He said and did a lot of things that seemed so revolutionarily different, so seemingly upside down and backward, but that in the end were rightside up and way out in front. When Jesus came to our planet, he came to show us what God is like. That mission alone made him wonderfully, sometimes unsettlingly, different.

And thank God that he is different!

Who would want God to come to our world and be just like us? Not me. I wouldn't be interested in a God who perpetuated our hellishly disappointing, broken ways of treating each other; who could gossip and slander like the best of them; who would use his power to take advantage of others, to demand that others serve him and live like life was always about him, to see women as pawns of masculine pleasure, to seek revenge on his enemies, or to point a wagging finger at us sinners!

Nor would I want a God who sat around twiddling his thumbs, worrying about whether or not he would make it in life, about whether or not life would be good to him.

As we have learned, when it comes to God, *Vive la différence!* And if we are followers of the Different One, then why are we so normal? Why does being different bother us? Why are we so much like everyone else?

Jesus died to liberate us from the curse of sameness and to recruit us to a new life—life with him in his emerging, victorious nation. He recruits us to be fellow revolutionaries in birthing his nation in our world, revolutionaries who will participate in the overthrow of the treacherous regime of the enemy, who will live in the freedom that Jesus brings, and who will live to set other captives free and welcome them to enjoy with us the wonderfully different rule of King Jesus.

As I'm wrapping up my work on this book, the Cubs are at it again. It's another season, and there is a lot of hope that *this could be the year.* But then, we've had that hope before. . . . Which reminds me of how privileged I am to be a part of the Jesus Nation—a nation in which all our hopes for a purposeful life and a bright, victorious future have been guaranteed by our champion, Jesus. Bewildered by life no more, as followers of Jesus we confidently take his nation forward by living to show through our lives the excellencies of the one who has called us out of darkness into his marvelous light. What a privilege! I will never cease to be amazed that he has seen fit by his grace to make me a part of the greatest nation ever . . . forever!

NOTES

Chapter 2: Something's Wrong

1. Peter Kreeft, *Everything You Ever Wanted to Know About Heaven but Never Dreamed of Asking* (Fort Collins, CO: Ignatius Press, 1990), 20.

Chapter 8: Will the Real Jesus Please Stand Up?

1. Douglas Coupland, *Life After God* (New York: Washington Square Press, 1995), 359.

Chapter 9: Life on Purpose

1. John G. Stackhouse Jr., *Making the Best of It* (Oxford: Oxford University Press, 2008), 19.

Chapter 11: Vive la Différence

1. Eugene Peterson, *The Jesus Way* (Grand Rapids: Eerdmans, 2007), 16–17.
2. Ibid., I.
3. Eric Sandras, *Buck-Naked Faith* (Colorado Springs: NavPress, 2004), 12–13.

Chapter 12: Excellence in Living

1. Alan M. Stibbs, "The First Epistle General of Peter," *The Tyndale New Testament Commentaries*, gen. ed. R. V. G. Tasher (Grand Rapids: Eerdmans, 1959), 104.
2. Ibid., 107–108
3. Matthew Parris, "As an Atheist, I Truly Belive Africa Needs God," *The Times Online*, http://www.timesonline.co.uk/tol/comment/columnists/matthew_parris/article5400568.ece.

Chapter 16: Jesus Our Champion

1. J. R. R. Tolkien, *The Fellowship of the Ring*, revised, authoritative edition (New York: Houghton Mifflin Company, 1965), 93.
2. I am indebted to Tim Keller of Redeemer Presbyterian Church in Manhattan for his insightful treatment of Jesus as Champion and for the supporting references to *The Lord of the Rings*.

Chapter 21: Marvelous Grace

1. This idea is found in C. K. Barrett, *The Gospel According to St. John* (London: SPCK, 1967), 138–139; and in Leon Morris, *The Gospel According to John*, revised (Grand Rapids: Eerdmans, 1995), 94–95.

ABOUT THE AUTHOR

DR. JOSEPH M. STOWELL serves as the eleventh president of Cornerstone University in Grand Rapids, Michigan. Comprised of approximately 2,500 undergraduate and graduate students, Cornerstone is a Christ-centered university with a passion for global influence through the transforming power of the gospel. The university is committed to creating an environment where students thrive both spiritually and intellectually as they prepare themselves to influence our world as followers of Jesus.

An internationally recognized conference speaker, Joe has also written several other books, including *The Trouble with Jesus*, *Simply Jesus and You*, *The Upside of Down*, and *Eternity*. Joe also serves with RBC Ministries, partnering in media productions, writing, and outreach to pastors. His "Strength for the Journey" Web ministry, www.getmorestrength.org, features daily devotionals, weekly messages and commentary, downloadable Bible study curriculum, and an audio library of his most-requested messages.

Joe serves on the boards of the Billy Graham Evangelistic Association and of Wheaton College and has a distinguished career in higher education and church leadership. He served as the president of Moody Bible Institute from 1987 to 2005 and as teaching pastor at the 10,000-member Harvest Bible Chapel in suburban Chicago from 2005 to early 2008, prior to assuming the presidency at Cornerstone University. He is a graduate of Cedarville University and of Dallas Theological Seminary and was honored with a doctorate of divinity degree from The Master's College in 1987. Joe and his wife, Martie, are the parents of three adult children and the grandparents of ten grandchildren.

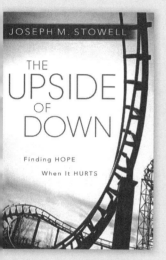
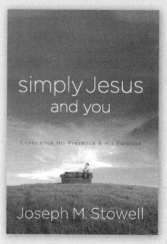